Words Their Way™

Word Sorts for Syllables and Affixes Spellers

D1319401

Francine Johnston
University of North Carolina, Greensboro

Marcia Invernizzi
University of Virginia

Donald R. Bear
University of Nevada, Reno

Shane Templeton
University of Nevada, Reno

PEARSON

Merrill
Prentice Hall

Upper Saddle River, New Jersey
Columbus, Ohio

Library of Congress Cataloging in Publication Data

Johnston, Francine R.
   Words their way : word sorts for syllables and affixes spellers / by Francine Johnston,
 Marcia Invernizzi, and Donald Bear.—1st ed.
      p. cm.
   ISBN 0-13-113592-9
      1. English language—Orthography and spelling—Problems, exercises, etc. 2. English
 language—Suffixes and prefixes—Problems, exercises, etc. 3. English
 language—Syllabication—Problems, exercises, etc. I. Invernizzi, Marcia. II. Bear, Donald
 R. III. Title.

PE1145.2.J63 2005
428.1'3—dc22

                                                                    2004040017

Vice President and Executive Publisher: Jeffery W. Johnston
Senior Editor: Linda Ashe Montgomery
Editorial Assistant: Laura Weaver
Development Editor: Hope Madden
Production Editor: Mary M. Irvin
Production Coordination: Amy Gehl, Carlisle Publishers Services
Design Coordinator: Diane C. Lorenzo
Cover Designer: Ali Mohrman
Cover image: Jean Claude Lejuene
Production Manager: Pamela D. Bennett
Director of Marketing: Ann Castel Davis
Marketing Manager: Darcy Betts Prybella
Marketing Coordinator: Tyra Poole

This book was set in Palatino by Carlisle Communications, Ltd. It was printed and bound by Courier
Kendallville, Inc. The cover was printed by Phoenix Color Corporation.

Pearson Education Ltd.   Pearson Education Australia Pty. Limited
Pearson Education Singapore Pte. Ltd. Pearson Education North Asia Ltd.
Pearson Education Canada, Ltd.   Pearson Educación de Mexico, S.A. de C.V.
Pearson Education—Japan   Pearson Education Malaysia Pte. Ltd.

10 9 8
ISBN: 0-13-113592-9

Contents

Preface

Words Their Way: Word Sorts for Syllables and Affixes Spellers is intended to complement the text *Words Their Way: Word Study for Phonics, Vocabulary, and Spelling Instruction*. That core text provides a practical, research-based, and classroom-proven way to study words with students. This companion text expands and enriches that word study, specifically for syllables and affixes spellers.

Syllables and affixes spellers are typically intermediate and advanced readers and writers. They have a foundation in common vowel patterns in single syllable words and are ready to study multi-syllabic words, beginning with consonant doubling and moving through the study of basic prefixes and suffixes.

Words Their Way: Word Sorts for Syllables and Affixes Spellers provides teachers with prepared reproducible sorts and step-by-step directions to guide students through the sorting lessons. There are organizational tips as well as follow-up activities to extend the lesson through weekly routines. The materials provided in this text will complement the use of any existing phonics, spelling, and reading curricula.

More resources for word study in the syllables and affixes stage, including additional spelling inventories for grades 3 through 8, resources for using word study with students who speak Spanish, links to websites related to word study, and news about the *Words Their Way* CD-ROM and Video, other companion materials, and word study events, can be found on the text's Companion Website. You can link to this site at

www.prenhall.com/bear

Overview

PLACEMENT

This collection of word sorts is for students who are in the syllables and affixes stage of spelling development and should already know how to spell the common and less common vowel patterns in single-syllable words covered in the within word pattern stage. Students in the syllables and affixes stage of development are usually in the upper elementary grades and middle school (grades 3–8). Students who are able to spell most one-syllable words correctly have the foundational knowledge needed to spell the base words to which affixes will be added (both suffixes and prefixes). They will also be ready to look for familiar vowel patterns in the two-syllable words they will study. It is important that students not begin the sorts in this collection until they have a firm foundation in vowel patterns. To figure out exactly where individual students should start you need to administer one of the spelling inventories described in Chapter 2 of *Words Their Way*.

ANALYTIC WORD STUDY

Word study as we describe it is analytic. Students examine words they already know how to read, and sometimes even spell, as a way to gain insight into how the spelling system works. This in turn enables them to analyze unfamiliar words they encounter in reading and to master the spelling of similar words. For this reason we do not recommend that you give a pretest and then eliminate all the correctly spelled words from the weekly routines and the final assessment. Known words provide important reference points for the student who is using, but confusing the spelling feature of interest. In this way we help students work from the known to the unknown through the scaffolding process. You may, however, want to use pretests at times to determine if students are appropriately placed in the word study sequence. Students are expected to spell about 50–75% of the words correctly on the pretest if the words and features are at their instructional level.

OVERVIEW OF CONTENT

This collection includes 55 sorts and is divided into 8 units with a total of over 1300 words. In the first set of sorts students will be exploring plural spellings (-s and -es) and how to add other inflected endings (-ed and -ing) to words using the "double, drop, or nothing" rules as well as the change *y* to *i* before certain suffixes rule. Two-syllable words will first be introduced through compound words, and then students will study the pattern of vowels and consonants at the place where syllables meet. We call these syllable juncture patterns. Next, the long-vowel patterns that students studied in the within word pattern stage will be reviewed in the stressed or accented syllable of two-syllable words. In a similar fashion *r*-influenced and ambiguous vowels (e.g., *oy*, *ou*, *au*, and *aw*) will also be re-examined in two-syllable words. After studying stressed syllables, students will look at the unstressed syllables that occur most commonly at the end of two-syllable words (e.g., *-el* or *-le*) and some of the unusual consonant sounds and spellings such as hard and soft *g* and *c*, *k*, *qu*, and silent consonants. Some one-syllable words will be revisited here. Affixes and root words are introduced next with prefixes (*re-*, *un-*, *dis-*, *pre-*, etc.) and suffixes (*-y*, *-ly*, *-ness*, *-ful*, etc.) that change the meaning and usage of words in fairly straightforward ways. The study of syllables and affixes anticipates the more complex roots and affixes that are explored extensively in the derivational relations stage. This collection of sorts ends with a look at homophones and homographs and words with three and four syllables.

The sorts in this collection present 24 words each week, a larger number than many basal spelling programs. The words have been selected according to their frequency of occurrence in reading materials for the elementary grades as well as for their spelling features. Students are expected to spell the 24 words in the sort and understand the spelling principles that the sorts reveal. Reducing the number of words to only 10 or 12 does not offer as many opportunities to discover spelling generalizations or to compare syllable juncture patterns and features. If you feel that 24 words are too many you can, in most cases, reduce the number to 21 by simply cutting off the last row of words. However, we believe that if students are appropriately placed and work with the words throughout the week, using the routines we recommend, 24 words are not too many, especially when they are grouped by spelling features. As mentioned above, if students are properly placed in the word study curriculum they should already be able to spell many of the words, so they will not be learning 24 completely new words in each lesson.

Each unit begins with *Notes for the Teacher* and suggestions you can use to introduce and practice the sorts. Sorts are presented as blackline masters that can be reproduced for every student to cut apart and use for sorting. (Enlarge these before making multiple copies to reduce cutting and waste.) Sorting is an essential instructional routine even for students in the upper grades who still enjoy the opportunity to manipulate words as they look for patterns and relationships among them. It is important that students sort their own words several times. You should also use the masters to prepare a set of words for modeling. You may want to make a transparency of the sort and cut it apart for use on an overhead or enlarge the words for use in a pocket chart. You can also simply make your own copy to cut apart and use on a desktop or on the floor. See Chapters 3 and 7 of *Words Their Way* 3^(rd) edition (*WTW*) and the *Words Their Way* CD-ROM (*WTWCD*) for additional background information, organizational tips, games, and activities. (All references to chapters and pages will be to the 3^(rd) edition. Earlier versions of *WTW* will have different chapter numbering and pages.)

INTRODUCING SORTS

Sorts can be introduced in a number of ways, and the way you choose will depend upon your own teaching style as well as the experience of your students. In *WTW* we describe **teacher-directed sorts, student-centered sorts,** and **guess my category sorts.** The sorts in this book are set up for teacher-directed sorts with the categories already established with headers and key words. These sorts work well when you are introducing a new unit or if you feel that your students need more explicit modeling and explanation. However, if you wish to make word sorting into more of a constructive process in which students discover the categories, you can cut off the headers before distributing the word sheets and use student-centered sorts as a way to begin. Guess my category sorts also engage the students in more active thinking. Cut off the headers but use the key words to establish the categories without giving away the feature characteristics of each category. (See *WTW* for more details on different sorting activities.)

PACING

The pacing for these sorts is designed for average growth. After introducing a sort you should spend about a week following routines that encourage students to practice for mastery. However, if your students seem to be catching on quickly you can speed up the pace by spending fewer days on a sort or you may skip some sorts altogether. On the other hand, you may need to slow down and perhaps even create additional sorts for some students. Although these sorts are arranged in a sequence that builds on earlier understandings there may be some cases in which you decide to use the sorts out of order. Some of the prefix sorts, for example, can be used earlier than what we present here. In general this collection of sorts might be considered the spelling curriculum for about a two-year period with time for extra sorts when needed or for review periods. Students' progress through these sorts should be carefully monitored with the goal of building a good foundation for the derivational relations stage to come.

Francine Johnston
Marcia Invernizzi
Donald Bear

SORTS 1-11

Plurals and Other Inflected Endings

NOTES FOR THE TEACHER

Inflected endings are a subcategory of suffixes that indicate tense (*walked, walking, walks*) and number (*cats, foxes*). Since the generalizations that govern the addition of inflected endings to single-syllable words are reliable and straightforward we refer to them as "rules." In order to apply the rules across a variety of words students will need an understanding of consonant and vowel patterns in the base word. (See page 227 in *WTW* for a complete listing of rules.) For this reason the first sort in this unit is a review of vowel patterns that will later determine whether one must drop the final *e* (VCe), double the final consonant (VC), or do nothing except add the ending (VVC, VCC). Since it is only the vowel and what follows that is of interest here, the onset or first few letters of the word (which can be one, two, or even three consonants) are not included in the pattern designation. Sorts 2, 3, 4, and 5 are designed to help students learn to identify base words and to see how the pattern in the base word must be considered before adding *-ing* and *-ed*. If you feel that your students only need a review you can skip sorts 1–3 and use only sorts 4 and 5. The words in sort 5 should also be sorted by the sound of *-ed* (/d/, /t/, /ed/) to help students see that this morphemic unit, which indicates past tense, is spelled the same despite changes in pronunciation. Sort 5 will help those students who might be spelling *walked* as WALKT as well as students who read *stopped* as *stop ped*. Sort 6 takes a look at irregular verbs that do not form the past tense by adding -ed (*sleep, slept; blow, blew*). There are many more of these words and students can be challenged to brainstorm others, find them in word hunts, and create a class list that can be added to over time.

Plurals are introduced in the within word pattern stage but are revisited here in different words. Sort 7 reviews the use of -es after certain consonants (*ch, sh, x,* and *s*) and also looks at how *es* adds another syllable to a word (*box-es, fenc-es*). Sort 8 examines words that form the plural in unusual ways such as *foot* and *feet* as well as words that end in *f* and change to *v* before adding *es* (*wife > wives*).

Final *y* generally represents the long *-i* sound in single-syllable words (*cry, try, fly*) and the long *-e* sound in two-syllable words (*many, hungry*). The final long *-e* sound can also be spelled with *-ey* or *-ie*. Sort 9 explores these *y*-endings before moving on to sorts 10 and 11, where rules that govern the changing of *y* to *i* before inflected endings are explored.

There are a number of ways that students can be introduced to inflected endings and some other sorts are suggested in *WTW* and on the *WTWCD*. Additional word lists in *WTW* can help you create more sorts if you think your students need extra practice. Since the inflected ending sorts are designed primarily to teach rules rather than particular words it is important to challenge students to apply the rules to words that are not in the sorts. For this reason transfer words are suggested for some of the sorts. Word hunts will be especially fruitful when students go looking for words that end in *-ing* and *-ed* in their reading materials. Words like *king* and *sing* might turn up in a word hunt and will give you the chance to reinforce the idea of base words.

STANDARD WEEKLY ROUTINES

1. **Repeated Work with the Words:** Each student should get his or her own copy of words to cut apart for sorting. We suggest that you enlarge the blackline masters so that no border is left around the words on the sheets the students receive. This will reduce waste paper and cutting time. After the sort has been modeled and discussed under the teacher's direction students should repeat the sort several times independently. The word cards can be stored in an envelope or plastic bag to be sorted again on other days and to take home to sort for homework. Chapter 3 in *WTW* contains tips for managing sorting and homework routines.

2. **Writing Sorts and Word Study Notebooks:** Students should record their word sorts by writing them into columns in their notebooks under the same key words that headed the columns of their word sort. An alternative is to use the homework form (word work at home) in the appendix. At the bottom of the writing sort, have your students **reflect** on and **declare** what they learned in that particular sort. This is especially important with the sorts in which students are learning rules about the addition of inflected endings. Ask them to write these rules in their own words.

3. **More Word Study Notebook Assignments:** You may want to assign additional words that provide practice and assess students' ability to **transfer** the rules to unstudied words. A list of transfer words follow many of the lessons in this unit. This is also a time when using the words in sentences is helpful. Students can be asked to use different forms of the word as in: *I like to walk. I walked to school yesterday and I am walking again today.* Chapter 3 in *WTW* has detailed descriptions of word study notebooks.

4. **Word Hunts:** Students should look for words in their daily reading that mirror the features studied in the weekly word sorts. Challenge them to find other words that contain the same patterns, endings, or unusual plural and past tense forms. After they find examples they can add the words to the bottom of the proper columns in their word study notebook. You may want to create posters or displays of all the words students can discover for each category. Sometimes generalizations can be made about the frequency of certain rules or features.

5. **No-Peeking or Blind Sorts:** A no-peeking or blind sort should be done only after students have had a chance to practice a sort several times. Headers or key words are laid down and students work together in a **buddy sort.** One student calls out a word without showing it. The other student points to where the word should go and the partner then shows the word card to check its spelling against the key word. In a no-peeking/blind **writing sort,** the student writes the word in the proper category using the key word as a model for spelling. After the word has been written, the partner calling the words shows the word card to the student doing the writing to check for correctness. These sorts require students to think about words by sound and by pattern and to use the key words as models for analogy. Buddy sorts are a great way to practice for spelling tests and can be assigned for homework.

6. **Games and Other Activities:** Create games and activities such as those in *WTW* or download them ready-made from the *WTWCD*. The *Racetrack Game* and the *Classic*

Card Game in Chapter 6 are good for a review of vowel patterns. *Double Scoop* and *Freddy the Hopping, Diving, Jumping Frog* in Chapter 7 are designed to reinforce inflected endings. *Double Scoop* can be downloaded from the *WTWCD*. *Memory* or *Concentration* would work especially well for the unusual plurals and verb forms that involve one-to-one matching.

7. **Assessment:** Students can be assessed by asking them to spell the words they have worked with over the week. You could call out only 10 or 15 of the 24 words as a spell check. After sorts that involve rules that generalize to many more words, you might want to call out a few transfer words to see if your students can spell their inflected forms. A Spell Check for this unit can be found on page 16. The spell check assesses students' retention of the particular words they have studied in this unit, and there is an additional spell check for transfer words.

SORT 1   REVIEW OF VOWEL PATTERNS IN ONE-SYLLABLE WORDS

Demonstrate

Prepare a set of words to use for teacher-directed modeling. Begin by going over the entire sheet of words to read and discuss the meanings of any unfamiliar words. You can do this by putting a transparency of the words on the overhead, by handing out the sheet of words to the students, or by going over the words on the cards one at a time.

Explain to your students that this is a review of vowel patterns they studied earlier. Introduce the headers CV, VCC, VVC, and VCe by pointing out that the *V* stands for a vowel and the *C* stands for a consonant. Model the sorting of the four boldface key words (*chief*, *wrap*, *smell*, and *whine*). Point out the consonant and vowel patterns in each word and, if you wish, underline those letters in the key words. Sort several more words, then begin to involve your students in the sorting process by showing a word and asking them where it should be placed. Continue with your students' help to sort all the words into columns under each header. The word *quit* may cause some confusion since the *u* is normally a vowel. In this word, however, it is part of the *qu* blend and represents the /w/ sound. Contrast *quit* with *bit* or *sit* to help students see that the vowel pattern is VC and not VVC. A similar confusion may occur with *quote*. Your final sort will look something like this:

VVC	VC	VCC	VCe
chief	**wrap**	**smell**	**whine**
fruit	twig	sharp	theme
brief	when	thank	brave
scout	plot	front	scale
clean	clog	climb	phone
stain	quit	trust	quote

Sort, Check, and Reflect

After modeling the sort have students cut apart and shuffle their cards and then sort using the same headers and key words. After the students sort, have them check their sorts by looking for the pattern in each column. If a student doesn't notice a mistake, guide her to it by saying: *One of these doesn't fit. See if you can find it.* Check to be sure *quit* ends up in the VC column. Encourage reflections by asking students how the words in each column are alike and how they are different from the other words. Students should note that the words under VC have short vowel sounds and the words under VCe have long vowel sounds. This can lead to a second sort of words by vowel sounds: short vowels, long vowels, and vowels that are neither long nor short (e.g., *scout* or *front*).

Extend

Have students store their words and pictures in an envelope or plastic bag so that they can reuse them throughout the week in individual and buddy sorts. Students should repeat the sort several times using the vowel pattern headers. See the list of standard weekly routines for follow-up activities to the basic sorting lesson. Some of the other sorts noted above might be assigned for written work in word study notebooks. Word hunts will turn up many more words that can be added to these categories.

SORT 2   ADDING *-ING* TO WORDS WITH VC AND VCC PATTERNS

Demonstrate

Students should find these words easy to read, so there is no reason to go over them in advance. Put up the headers VC and VCC. Pull out the base words and have the students help you sort them into two categories starting with *get* and *ask*. Explain that these are *base words*. Ask if there is anything they notice about all the base words (e.g., they all have one vowel that is usually short; they are all verbs.). Then match the *-ing* form of the word to each base word. Ask the students what happened to the base word *get* before the *-ing* was added. Repeat with several more words in the column. Introduce the term "double" and explain that when a base word ends in one vowel and one consonant we must double the final consonant before adding *-ing*. Put the header *double* above the word *getting*. Then ask what they notice about the *-ing* words in the other column and ask them why this might be so. Guide them to notice that the *-ing* was just added without any change. Add the header *nothing*. The final sort will look something like this:

VC	double	VCC	nothing
get	getting	ask	asking
swim	swimming	yell	yelling
run	running	rest	resting
sit	sitting	stand	standing
put	putting	pass	passing
		jump	jumping
		pick	picking

Sort, Check, and Reflect

After modeling the sort with the group have students repeat the sort under your supervision using the same headers and key words. Have them check their sort by looking for the pattern in each column. Encourage the students to reflect by asking them how the words in each column are alike and what they have learned about adding *-ing* to base words. Have the students put the rules into their own words. You may want to write down this rule on chart paper and post it for reference. Leave space for the additional rules and revisions that will develop over the weeks to come.

Extend

Students should repeat this sort several times and work with the words using some of the weekly routines listed above. Word hunts will turn up lots of words that can be added to these categories, but students will find many words that do not fit either of them. Tell your students to add these words to a third column (oddballs) and challenge them to see if they can discover the rule that governs these other words in anticipation of the sort for next week.

Students might be encouraged to write contrasting sentences for the base word and its -ing form: *I swim on a team. I have been swimming for three years.* Ask students to share sentences using the -ing form and ask them if they notice anything (using -ing as a verb often requires helping verbs such as *am, have been, was,* etc.).

Give students additional words and ask them to apply the rule. Some suggested transfer words are: *drip, hunt, tug, kick, stir, mop, wink, quit, wish, sob, guess, smell.*

SORT 3   ADDING -ING TO WORDS WITH VCe AND VVC PATTERNS

Demonstrate

Introduce this sort in a manner similar to sort 2. Ask the students what happened to the base word *use* before the -ing was added. Look at the other words under the VCe header to see how the e is missing in each inflected word. Introduce the term "e-drop" and put it at the top of the column. Explain that when a base word ends in silent e we must drop the e before adding -ing. Guide students to notice that the -ing was just added without any change to the VVC words. The sort will look something like this.

VCe	e-drop	VVC	nothing
use	using	eat	eating
close	closing	moan	moaning
write	writing	dream	dreaming
wave	waving	meet	meeting
trade	trading	clean	cleaning
skate	skating	mail	mailing

Sort, Check, Reflect, and Extend

Students should repeat the sort using the same headers and key words. Encourage the students to reflect by asking them how the words in each column are alike and what they have learned about adding -ing to base words. Review what they learned in the previous sort and add to the chart. Give students additional words and ask them to apply the rule. Some suggested transfer words are: *ride, need, give, bake, peek, smile, vote, bloom, scream, joke, join, shout.*

SORT 4   INFLECTED ENDINGS: REVIEW OF DOUBLE, E-DROP, AND NOTHING

Explain to students that they will review adding -ing to base words this week. You might let students do this sort as a student-centered sort. For a teacher-directed sort put up the headers *double, e-drop,* and *nothing.* Place the key words *setting, hiking,* and *reading* under each header. Ask the students to identify the base word in each key word and then to determine what was done to the base word before the *-ing* was added. You may want to underline the base word in each key word. Sort one more word under each key word and then sort the rest of the words with student help. *Fixing* should be under "nothing" for right now:

double	e-drop	nothing	oddball
setting	**hiking**	**reading**	
cutting	moving	adding	
stopping	living	spelling	
begging	coming	floating	
grinning	having	feeling	
jogging	taking	talking	
humming		pushing	
		fixing*	
		working	
		chewing	
		snowing	

*This will become an oddball after the second sort.

Guide the students to reflect on how the words in each column are alike. They may notice that the base words under "double" have the VC pattern and those under "*e*-drop" have the VCe pattern. However, under "nothing" there are a number of different patterns. These can be sorted out in a second sort. Headers are not provided, but you can create them if you feel they are needed. A second sort will look something like this:

VVC	VCC	oddball
reading	spelling	snowing
floating	talking	chewing
feeling	pushing	fixing
	adding	
	working	

The words *chewing, snowing,* and *fixing* should raise questions. While *chewing* and *snowing* might appear to be VC words that require doubling, the final *w* does not double because it is acting as part of a vowel pattern rather than as a consonant. *Fixing* does have the VC pattern but does not double. This is a rare exception to the rule. Have students think of other words that end in *x* such as *box* or *mix*. Show them that these words do not double because double *x* is not a pattern that occurs in English (*x* represents the blend of two letters: $k + s$). This sort will take some discussion but ultimately what we want students to see is that in most cases the *-ing* is simply added to the word and it is only when a word fits the VC or VCe pattern that a change to the base word is needed.

Sort, Check, and Reflect

After modeling the sorts have students repeat the first sort using the headers "double," "*e*-drop," or "nothing." The only real oddball is *fixing* because it does not double as expected. To reinforce the idea of base words you might ask students to underline them. Help the students articulate a rule that covers all the words. This may be a revision to former rules.

Extend

You might sort all the words from lessons 2, 3, and 4 by "double, *e*-drop, or nothing" as a review. Students should look back at word hunts from the previous weeks to find oddball words they can now sort into one of the three categories. (Even words like *going, see-*

ing, flying, studying, etc., which have patterns different from the ones included in these sorts, can go under "nothing.")

Give students additional words and ask them to apply the rules. Some suggested transfer words are: *slip, row, sneeze, pout, hunt, mix, tap, cheer, love, speed, dress, start, box, draw, win.*

SORT 5   ADDING -*ED* TO WORDS WITH DOUBLE, *E*-DROP, AND NO CHANGE

Demonstrate, Sort, Check, and Reflect

You might begin this sort by asking your students to spell *hopped* and then *hoped*. Ask them to justify why they spelled these words as they did and see if they can generalize from what they learned from the -*ing* sorts. Explain that students often have trouble with these words and that the sort for this week will help them learn and remember the rules that govern the addition of -*ed* just as they did for -*ing*. Students can sort without the headers for a student-centered sort, or you can begin a teacher-directed sort using the headers. Asking students to underline the base word may be helpful in determining patterns, especially in words like *hoped* and *saved*. Help the students see that the rules are similar to the rules for adding -*ing* and can be summed up as "double, drop, or nothing." Talk about the fact that adding -*ed* means that something has already happened and that such words are said to be in the "past tense."

VC	VCe	VVC	VCC	oddball
hopped	**hoped**	**joined**	**acted**	mixed
planned	saved	waited	wanted	
grabbed	closed	seemed	helped	
nodded	liked	shouted	started	
stepped	lived		hunted	
dropped	named		passed	
			called	

Extend

Challenge your students to sort these words in a second sort by the sound of the -*ed* ending as shown below. No headers are provided for this sort but are indicated here for clarity. Ask students if they can see any letter patterns in the base words in each column. They might notice that certain consonants precede certain sounds (*p* before /t/, *d* and *t* before /ed/) and that the words in the last column have added a syllable to the base word.

/t/	/d/	/id/
hopped	planned	nodded
stepped	grabbed	waited
dropped	moved	shouted
hoped	closed	acted
liked	loved	wanted
helped	named	started
passed	saved	hunted
	lived	
	joined	
	seemed	
	called	

Ask students to apply their knowledge by adding -*ed* to additional words: *march, tame, beg, clean, wave, boil, clip, name, mail, scoop, stir, talk, climb, snap, melt, score, show, thaw, chew, pet.*

SORT 6   UNUSUAL PAST TENSE WORDS

Demonstrate, Sort, Check, and Reflect

Most of these words are not hard to spell, but this sort will help students see that not all verbs form the past tense by adding -*ed*. This may be an especially helpful sort for students whose native language is not English. Introduce the sort by putting up the headers and matching the present and past tenses of each verb as shown below. Explain that these words are called "irregular verbs."

present	past
sleep	**slept**
keep	kept
slide	slid
shine	shone
freeze	froze
draw	drew
sweep	swept
drive	drove
bleed	bled
know	knew
throw	threw
say	said

Extend

Challenge your students to come up with a way to sort the pairs of words into categories that reflect the kind of change that was made to the word. Here is a possible sort:

slide slid	shine shone	know knew	sleep slept	say said
bleed bled	drive drove	throw threw	keep kept	
	freeze froze	draw drew	sweep swept	

Students should describe the categories in their own way and brainstorm additional words that could be added in each one. Some additional words that could be added to the sort include: *feed/fed, meet/met, choose/chose, write/wrote, drink/drank, rise/rose, ride/rode, grow/grew, catch/caught, seek/sought, pay/paid, lay/laid, forget/forgot* and so on. (The past tenses of *lay, pay,* and *say* are all formed the same way (*laid, paid, said*), so maybe *said* is not so strange after all!) There are many irregular verbs, and students might set aside a part of their word study notebook to add others over time. For a complete list check the Internet. One source is *http://www.englishpage.com/irregularverbs/irregularverbs.html.*

SORT 7   PLURAL ENDINGS: ADDING -*ES*

Demonstrate

Be sure the students can read the words and know the meaning of each. Remind students that to make a word plural either -*s* or -*es* is added. Sort the words first by these two headers. Students will need to think about the base word in order to make this distinction. Since all the words end in -*es* we recommend underlining the base word. Read the words in columns and point out that adding -*es* also adds another syllable (except for *gloves*). This additional syllable make these words fairly easy to spell.

Push the words that simply added -*s* to the side and ask students what they notice about the base words in the words that are left. Focus their attention on the last one or two letters. Model the next step of the sort by placing *benches, brushes, foxes,* and *guesses* into separate categories. Create headers for these if you want by underlining the *ch* in *benches*, the *sh* in *brushes*, and so on, or by creating headers like the ones below. After completing the sort as shown below ask students how the words in each column are alike. Help students articulate a rule (Add *-es* to words that end in *ch, sh, x,* and *s*) and add it to the class chart. Since adding *-es* to make a word plural adds another syllable /ez/ to the word students do not have too much difficulty spelling the plural form.

add *-es*				add *-s*
-ch	*-sh*	*-x*	*-s*	
benches	brushes	foxes	guesses	**gloves**
speeches	splashes	mixes	kisses	horses
scratches	crashes			voices
churches	ashes			changes
peaches	eyelashes			places
sketches	leashes			
ditches				
branches				
watches				

Extend

Give students transfer words to practice applying the rules: *switch, house, glass, tray, choice, witch, song, flame, hamster, smash, fix, mess, shape, lunch, sandwich, grade, wish, class, drink, mask.*

SORT 8   UNUSUAL PLURALS

Explain to your students that just as with irregular verbs, some words form plurals in unusual ways. Begin this sort by matching singular and plural forms. Take it further by introducing the headers and sorting pairs of words into those that end in *f* and form the plural by changing the *f* to *v* and adding *-es* and those that make a change in the vowel. There are also words like *deer* and *sheep* that can represent either singular or plural.

fe > ves		vowel change		no change
wife	**wives**	**foot**	**feet**	**sheep**
leaf	leaves	woman	women	deer
loaf	loaves	mouse	mice	
life	lives	tooth	teeth	
wolf	wolves	goose	geese	
knife	knives			

Extend

Students may have a hard time finding more of these unusual plurals in a word hunt, but some others include: *halves, calves, shelves, elves, ourselves, scarves, man/men, fish, children.* Some of these might be assigned as transfer words. Students can be asked to write the plural of *half, calf, shelf, elf,* and *scarf* to apply what they have learned.

SORT 9   FINAL Y

Go over the words to be sure that the students can read and understand them. Next, ask your students what they notice about the words (e.g., many end in the letter *y*; most end with the long *-e* sound). Introduce the headers and model the sort starting with the key words. Point out to your students that the slash marks around a letter indicate its sound (e.g.,/e/ represents the long -*e* sound). You may want to do this as a student-centered sort and let your students identify the categories. If the students put all the words ending in *y* together, ask them to read the words aloud to hear the sound at the end and put those in a new column.

-y = /e/	-ey = /e/	-ie = /e/	-y = /i/
many	**turkey**	**movie**	**July**
hungry	money	cookie	rely
fifty	honey	goalie	try
ready	jockey		
angry	chimney		
every	hockey		
ugly			
very			
body			
plenty			
twenty			
empty			

SORT 10   Y PLURALS

Demonstrate, Sort, Check, and Reflect

The sort for this week introduces the "change *y* to *i* and add *es*" rule. There are not a lot of common words that follow these rules, but some of the words that do are of high frequency and often pose spelling challenges. Begin the sort by going over the words and asking how they are alike (they are all plurals). Put up the key words *plays* and *cities*, ask the students for the base word spelling of each, and write it below the word. Model sorting several more words in the same manner and then have your students help sort.

Since the spelling of the base word is somewhat obscured when the *y* is changed to *i*, ask students to write the base word below the word to help them see the pattern. Ask the students what they notice about the base word (words like *plays* have a vowel before the final *y* but words like *city* have a consonant). Explain that the rule for plurals that end in *y* is to change the *y* to *i* and add *es*, but not if the word has a vowel before the *y*. Add the new rule to your chart. Show your students what *plays* would look like if the *y* was changed to an *i* (*plaies*). Such a spelling involves three vowels in a row, and this is rare in English. Add the headers to the sort at this point and have the students use the headers when they sort for themselves.

+ s	y > i + es
plays	**cities**
monkeys	babies
alleys	ponies
valleys	stories
trays	parties
boys	ladies
toys	fireflies
donkeys	candies
journeys	duties
	armies
	berries
	families

SORT 11   INFLECTED ENDINGS (-*ED* AND -*ING*) ADDED TO WORDS THAT END IN *Y*

Demonstrate, Sort, Check, and Reflect

Review the previous sort by writing up the word *cry* and asking students how you would make it into the word *cries*. Explain that *cries* here is not the plural of the word *cry* but a different verb form, as in: *The baby often cries when he is lonely.* Explain that this week you will be looking at how to add -*s*, -*ed*, and -*ing* to verbs that end in *y*. Introduce the headers and sort the three forms of the word *cry: crying, cries, cried.* Ask for the base word and underline it in *crying.* Sort the rest of the words in a similar manner. After sorting ask your students what they notice about each column of words. Pull out *enjoys* and *stays.* Talk about how they are different from the other words under +*s*, which changed the *y* to *i*. Connect this to the study of plurals in the previous lesson noting that these words have a vowel before the *y*. In a similar manner pull out *enjoyed* and *stayed* after talking about how the words under -*ed* changed the *y* to *i* before adding -*ed*. Help your students form a rule to add to the class list. Talk about why you would not change the *y* to *i* before adding -*ing* (the words would look like *criing* and *i* very rarely doubles in English (except in *skiing* and *Hawaiian*)).

+ *ing*	+ *s*	+ *ed*
crying	**cries**	**cried**
replying	replies	replied
studying	studies	studied
copying	copies	copied
carrying	carries	carried
hurrying	hurries	hurried
enjoying	enjoys	enjoyed
staying	stays	stayed

Extend

Check for transfer with these words: *fly, stray, rely, spray, try.*

REVIEW

After many sorts that focus on base words and inflected endings your chart of rules may look quite complicated. Now is the time to review and simplify it. The following are really the only rules students need to remember, for now, that cover most cases:

> **DOUBLE:** When a word ends in one vowel and one consonant you **double** the consonant before adding -*ed* and -*ing*.
> **E-DROP:** When a word ends in *e* you **drop** the *e* before adding -*ing* and -*ed*.
> **CHANGE y to i:** When a word ends in a consonant and a *y* you **change the y to i** before adding -*ed* or -*es*.
> **NOTHING:** Otherwise, just **do nothing** and add the ending.
> **ADD es:** to make words plural that end in *s, sh, ch,* or *x*.

Students can review all of these rules by sorting words from previous sorts into these categories. This is a good time to play games that will reinforce these rules such as *Double Scoop* and *Freddy the Hopping, Diving, Jumping Frog* described in *WTW*. Adapt this game to review all of the rules.

SPELL CHECK 1 ASSESSMENT FOR INFLECTED ENDINGS (-S, -ED, -ING)

Retention Test: The words below have been selected from previous lessons. (You may want to use different ones.) Call them aloud for students to spell on a sheet of note-book paper:

1. swimming	6. stayed	11. leaves
2. eating	7. dropped	12. monkeys
3. copies	8. foxes	13. named
4. living	9. helped	14. cookie
5. fixing	10. spelling	15. studying

Transfer Test: Students should be expected not only to spell words from previous sorts but also to apply their understanding of how to add inflected endings to base words. In this assessment students will be asked to add -s, -ed, and -ing to given base words. A prepared assessment can be found on page 28. The final work should look as follows:

Base word	Add s or es	Add ed	Add ing
1. trip	trips	tripped	tripping
2. chase	chases	chased	chasing
3. need	needs	needed	needing
4. dress	dresses	dressed	dressing
5. dry	dries	dried	drying
6. tax	taxes	taxed	taxing
7. fan	fans	fanned	fanning
8. race	races	raced	racing
9. play	plays	played	playing

VVC	VC	VCC	VCe
chief	wrap		smell
whine	fruit		twig
sharp	theme		brief
when	thank		brave
scout	plot		front
scale	clean		clog
climb	phone		stain
quit	trust		quote

VC	VCC	double	nothing
get	getting		ask
asking	swim		yell
swimming	rest		run
sit	yelling		resting
stand	running		pass
sitting	pick		standing
jump	put		picking
putting	passing		jumping

Words Their Way: Word Sorts for Syllables and Affixes Spellers © 2005 by Prentice-Hall, Inc.

VCe	VVC	*e*-drop	nothing
use		**using**	**eat**
eating	close		moan
wave	writing		dreaming
meeting	dream		skate
closing	trading		cleaning
clean	write		moaning
trade	skating		waving
meet	mail		mailing

Words Their Way: Word Sorts for Syllables and Affixes Spellers © 2005 by Prentice-Hall, Inc.

double	*e*-drop	nothing	oddball
setting	hiking	reading	
floating	cutting	moving	
stopping	living	spelling	
coming	begging	adding	
grinning	having	feeling	
jogging	taking	talking	
pushing	humming	working	
fixing	chewing	snowing	

SORT 5 Adding *-ed* to Words with Double, *E*-Drop and No Change

VC	VCe	VVC	VCC
hopped	hoped		joined
acted	planned		saved
waited	wanted		grabbed
closed	mixed		helped
nodded	liked		shouted
started	hunted		stepped
named	passed		dropped
called	lived		seemed

present	past	
sleep	slept	throw
slide	drive	slid
drew	threw	shine
shone	freeze	sweep
bleed	keep	bled
froze	draw	drove
say	swept	said
know	kept	knew

add *es*	add *s*	
benches	gloves	foxes
guesses	brushes	speeches
splashes	scratches	horses
mixes	churches	crashes
voices	peaches	eyelashes
kisses	sketches	ditches
leashes	changes	branches
watches	places	ashes

fe > ves	Vowel Change	no change
wife	wives	sheep
foot	feet	loaf
lives	women	leaves
leaf	geese	woman
mouse	loaves	life
wolves	mice	goose
knives	knife	wolf
tooth	deer	teeth

-y = /e/	-ey = /e/	-ie = /e/	-y = /i/
many	turkey	movie	
July	hungry	money	
fifty	ready	angry	
honey	cookie	rely	
every	jockey	ugly	
very	body	goalie	
try	plenty	twenty	
empty	hockey	chimney	

+ s	y > i + es	
plays	cities	babies
ponies	monkeys	alleys
stories	parties	ladies
valleys	trays	fireflies
candies	duties	armies
toys	berries	boys
families	journeys	donkeys

Words Their Way: Word Sorts for Syllables and Affixes Spellers © 2005 by Prentice-Hall, Inc.

+*ing*	+*s*	+*ed*
crying	cries	cried
replying	copying	carrying
studying	stays	replied
enjoying	copied	studies
replies	carries	enjoys
stayed	staying	studied
copies	carried	enjoyed
hurrying	hurries	hurried

Transfer Test #1 for Sorts 1-11

Directions: Add the ending to the base word. Don't forget to look at the pattern and spelling of the base word to determine what changes might be needed.

Base word	Add *s or es*	Add *ed*	Add *ing*
1. trip			
2. chase			
3. need			
4. dress			
5. dry			
6. tax			
7. fan			
8. race			
9. play			

Words Their Way: Word Sorts for Syllables and Affixes Spellers © 2005 by Prentice-Hall, Inc.

SORTS 12-13

Compound Words

NOTES FOR THE TEACHER

Check out *WTW* for a section on compound words under the syllables and affixes activity section (page 234). Compound words show up early in children's reading and teachers should be able to talk about such words when they arise. Spelling compound words is not especially challenging **if** students know how to spell the two words that make up the compound word. For this reason we leave the formal study of compound words to the early syllables and affixes stage when students have mastered the patterns in one-syllable words. By doing it here we want to reinforce the idea that there are familiar parts within longer words that will make those words easier to understand, read, and spell— some of the key understandings of this stage.

We offer only two sorts here in this short unit, one made up of some words that are concrete and easy to spell and another that contains a collection of less concrete high-frequency words. This should be enough to introduce the term "compound words" and to get your students attuned to looking for them in later sorts and in the reading and writing they do all the time. Students can be challenged to set apart a section of their word study notebooks to record more compound words they might find (the list of compound words in the Appendix of *WTW* is only a small sample), or the class might create a bulletin board or chart that is added to during the entire year. Hyphenated words might be added as well since these are often confused with compound words. (Is it *goodbye* or *good-bye*?) The dictionary can help out here. No spell check is included for this short unit.

Check out Rick Walton's list of more than 2,000 compound words at www.rickwalton.com/curricul/compound.htm

STANDARD WEEKLY ROUTINES FOR USE WITH SORTS 12-13

1. **Repeated Sorts, Writing Sorts, and Word Study Notebooks:** Students should sort their words independently or with a buddy and record their sorts by writing them into columns in their notebooks.
2. **Draw:** Students often enjoy illustrating the meaning of both the words that make up the compound words as well as the final word (*snow* + *man* = *snowman*). Ask your students to pick five words and draw a picture that will make the meaning clear. Such drawings might be displayed or collected into a class book.
3. **Word Hunts:** Rather than hunting for words that fit the specific categories established with the words in the sort (e.g., more words with *light*), word hunts can focus on finding any compound words.

4. **Brainstorming:** Give students one word (like *man*) and challenge them to come up with as many compound words as possible (*manmade, manhole, manhandle,* etc.).

5. **Games and Other Activities:** *Word Study Scattergories,* described in Chapter 6 (page 208) of *WTW,* can make the brainstorming described above into a game using these suggested words: *man, air, back, eye, hand, foot, home, horse, house, land, life, night, out, over, play, road, sand, sea, under, water,* and *wind*. You might also create a version of *Win, Lose, or Draw,* described in Chapter 6, that features compound words.

SORT 12   COMPOUND WORDS

Demonstrate

This is a good collection of words to use for a student-centered sort. Show your students all the words without going over the meanings in advance (that will come later). Ask them for ideas about how to sort these words into categories. Students should quickly spot the common elements, but if they do not, be ready to model each category. Note that the word *headlight* can be sorted in two different places. Review the term "compound words" with your students and help them develop their own definition based on the words they see in the sort. After sorting, discuss the meaning of some of the words and how the meaning relates to the two words that make it up: *A bookmark marks your place in a book; Sunlight is the light that comes from the sun,* and so on. Some compound words cannot be interpreted so literally. *Headstrong* does not literally mean *strong in the head* but rather *strong willed*. Ask students to look up the meaning of a few words such as this one as part of the group discussion. The sort will look something like this:

bookcase	**light**house	**down**hill	**head**ache	**snow**man
bookmark	lightweight	downstairs	headfirst	snowflake
bookworm	daylight	downtown	headlight	snowstorm
cookbook	flashlight	downpour	headphones	snowplow
scrapbook	sunlight	countdown	headstrong	
	(headlight)			

Sort, Check, and Reflect

Have students shuffle their words and repeat the sort under your supervision. Ask students to identify the parts of words that might be hard to spell such as the *ache* in *headache* or the *weight* in *lightweight*. Have them check their sorts by looking for or underlining the word part that is shared by all the words in each column. Encourage the students to reflect and declare their understanding of what a compound word is.

Extend

Have students think of other words that share these same word parts. Some include: *bookkeeper, textbook, downstream, download, downcast, downfall, headband, headway, headline, snowdrift, snowshoe, snowball*.

SORT 13   HIGH-FREQUENCY COMPOUND WORDS

Demonstrate, Sort, Check, and Reflect

This collection features high-frequency compound words that are not so easy to define. Rather than ask students the meaning of the words ask them to use them in sentences.

Introduce this sort in a manner similar to sort 11. Some words may be sorted in more than one place, as shown by those in parentheses below:

some**body**	him**self**	any**one**	every**thing**	with**out**	in**side**
something	themselves	everyone	anything	outside	beside
sometime	yourself	(someone)	nothing	throughout	sideways
somewhere	herself		(something)	checkout	
somehow	myself				
someone	itself				

Extend

Have students think of other words that share these same word parts. Some include: *someday, plaything, blackout, blowout, cookout, hideout, outfit, checkout, timeout, outfield, outlaw, outlast, outline, outlive, everywhere, everyplace, hillside.* Point out the plural of *self* in *themselves* to review adding *s* to words that end in *v.* Ask students to look for any compound words they can find when doing a word hunt rather than looking for more words with these same word parts.

bookcase	lighthouse	snowman
headache	downhill	headphones
downstairs	headfirst	bookmark
snowflake	downtown	daylight
flashlight	bookworm	downpour
snowstorm	headlight	cookbook
scrapbook	sunlight	countdown
snowplow	headstrong	lightweight

<u>so</u>mebody	him<u>self</u>	every<u>thing</u>
any<u>one</u>	with<u>out</u>	in<u>side</u>
something	themselves	everyone
outside	anything	beside
sometime	yourself	throughout
sideways	somewhere	herself
nothing	somehow	someone
myself	checkout	itself

Syllable Juncture

NOTES FOR THE TEACHER

"Syllable juncture" is a term used to describe the point at which two syllables join. The pattern of vowels and consonants that meet at this point sends cues to the reader about the likely point of division that might be useful in decoding an unfamiliar word. Learning about the patterns of vowels and consonants on either side of the syllable juncture helps spellers, too. For example, spellers will face decisions such as whether to put one or two consonants in the middle of a word (e.g., is it *dinner* or *diner*?). Knowledge of syllable juncture patterns is therefore a useful tool for analyzing the longer words readers and spellers will encounter.

There are a number of syllable patterns that occur at the juncture and these are referred to as syllable types. The ones that are covered in these four sorts include open and closed syllables and their variations: VCV, VCCV, VCCCV, VVCV, and VV. The other syllable types will be covered in the study of vowel patterns in stressed syllables that follows. The most reliable pattern of vowels and consonants is the VCCV pattern in words such as *supper* and *winter*. The VCCV pattern regularly signals that the first syllable is closed with a short vowel sound. A variation of the VCCV pattern is the closed VCCCV pattern as in *tumble*.

The VCV pattern most often represents the open syllable with a long-vowel sound in the first syllable, as in *super* and *diner*, when the syllable is split after the long vowel (V/CV) and left "open." However, there are also a number of words in which the syllable division comes after the consonant (VC/V), as in *wagon* where the first syllable is closed with a consonant and the vowel sound is short. Variations of the open-syllable pattern are the VVCV pattern in *reason* and the VV pattern in *create*. While you can introduce and use the terms "open" and "closed" when referring to syllables it might be best to focus on the pattern of vowels and consonants at the syllable juncture. You undoubtedly have intuitive knowledge about syllables, but you will learn along with your students as that knowledge is made explicit through these sorts.

The words selected for sorts 14–16 are among the most frequent two-syllable words and should be easy to read by students in the early syllables and affixes stage. You will see that many more are listed in the Appendix of *WTW* and you might use these lists to develop more sorts and sorts with more challenging words. The words in sort 17 are not as common, but this is a logical place to introduce and contrast the patterns.

STANDARD WEEKLY ROUTINES FOR USE WITH SORTS 14–18

1. **Repeated Sorts, Writing Sorts, and Word Study Notebooks:** Students should sort their words independently and with a buddy (no-peeking or blind sorts) and record

their sorts by writing them into columns in their notebooks or on the homework form in the appendix. See *WTW* for details about different kinds of sorts and word study notebooks.

2. **Break Words into Syllables:** Throughout this unit students will be thinking about how words are broken into syllables. They can be asked to indicate syllable division in their word study notebooks as they write the words: *su-per* or *su/per*.

3. **Word Hunts:** Students will find many words in their daily reading that mirror the featured syllable patterns in sorts 13, 14, and 15 and these can be added to the bottom of the proper columns in their word study notebook. It will be more difficult to find words that fit the patterns in sort 16, so you may want to skip word hunts for that lesson.

4. **Games and Other Activities:** The card game of *Match* described in Chapter 5 of *WTW* and the *Classic Card Game* and *Word Study Uno* in Chapter 6 are just some of the games that can be adapted for syllable patterns. Card games are popular with students in the middle elementary grades and any game that has 4–5 categories can be adapted to review these syllable features.

5. **Assessment:** To assess students' weekly mastery, ask them to spell the words in a standard spelling test format. You can also ask the students to set up their paper with headers and write the words under the correct columns. It is not necessary to assess all 24 words. Students will need to be prepared to spell any of the words you select. A final Spell Check will assess retention of the words in all four sorts.

SORT 14   SYLLABLE JUNCTURE IN VCV AND VCCV PATTERNS

Demonstrate

You might introduce this lesson by asking your students to spell *super* and *supper*. Ask them to explain why they spelled the words as they did. Assure them that the sort you are doing that week will help them understand what is going on with such words. Explain to your students that you will be looking at patterns in a different way and introduce the headers VCV and VCCV. Put the key words *super* and *supper* under the headers and explain how the letters in the headers refer only to the pattern of vowels and consonants in the middle of the word where two syllables come together. Underline the letters in the words and label them: VCV represents the *u*, *p*, and *e* in *super*, while VCCV represents the *u*, *p*, *p*, and *e* in *supper*. Notice that one or more letters, or no letters, can come on either side of the juncture. Sort several more words, then begin to involve your students in the sorting process by showing them a word and asking them where it should be placed. Continue with your students' help to sort all the words into columns under each header. For now the oddball *busy*, which has the pattern but not the long sound of *u*, should be sorted under VCV.

Now read down the VCV column of words and ask your students to listen to the vowel sound in the first syllable. They should notice that in each word the vowel sound is long except for the word *busy*. Move this word to the oddball category. Explain that these first syllables that end with a long-vowel sound are called "open." You might demonstrate how to break words into two syllables by drawing a line between the two syllables, as in *su/per*. Remind them that they have studied open syllables in words that end with a vowel such as *go*, *row*, and *blue*. Next, read the VCCV column to find that the vowel is short in the first syllable. Again you might draw a line between the syllables (*sup/per*) and explain that these syllables are called "closed" because the short-vowel sound is "closed" with a consonant. Remind them of words such as *fled*, *drag*, *trip*, and *stop* that have the VC pattern. Your final sort will look something like this:

VCV	VCCV	oddball
super	**supper**	busy
diner	dinner	
tiger	happy	
later	pretty	
paper	penny	
even	puppy	
over	rabbit	
ruler	kitten	
crazy	hello	
open	letter	
tiny	lesson	
	summer	

Sort, Check, and Reflect

After modeling the sort have students repeat the sort with your guidance. To reinforce the idea of the syllables you might ask them to draw a line between them or they could do this in their word study notebooks. Have them check their sorts by looking for the pattern in each column. Encourage the students to reflect by asking them how the words in each column are alike and what they have learned. Help the students to articulate a generalization such as, "A syllable that ends in a vowel usually has a long-vowel sound, and a syllable that ends in a consonant usually has a short-vowel sound. "

Extend

Students should work with the words using some of the weekly routines listed above. A word hunt will turn up many words as well as oddballs that will foreshadow other sorts to come. Have them put oddballs into a third column and keep them handy for further reference. Review forming plurals with words that end in *y* by asking students to spell *puppies* and *pennies*.

SORT 15   MORE SYLLABLE JUNCTURE IN VCV AND VCCV PATTERNS

This sort reinforces the patterns from the previous sort, but adds VCC words that have different consonants at the juncture (basket) to contrast with the words that have the same consonant at the juncture or "doublets" (happen). This sort can be introduced in a manner similar to sort 13, or students can be asked to determine the categories for themselves in a student-centered sort. Students might go back to the word hunt from the last sort to find words that fit in this new category.

VCV	VCCV (doublet)	VCCV (different)	oddball
silent	**happen**	**basket**	water
female	matter	winter	
stupid	follow	problem	
fever	butter	number	
moment	yellow	finger	
	pattern	sister	
	bottom	chapter	
	pillow	member	
		blanket	
		window	

SORT 16   SYLLABLE JUNCTURE IN VCV AND VVCV PATTERNS

The VCV pattern is most often the open syllable with a long-vowel sound as in *hu-man*, but there are also many common words in which VCV has a closed syllable, as in *wag-on*. Explain how the headers V/CV and VC/V indicate this. The VVCV juncture pattern is a variation of the open-syllable pattern since the syllable still ends with a vowel that has the long vowel sound. Introduce this sort in a way similar to sorts 14 and 15. Ask students to revisit earlier word hunts to find words that might fit the new categories established here. Speculate about why the letter *V* might not be doubled in words like *river*, *never*, and *seven*. Write these words with a double *V* and notice how the two *V*'s begin to look like a *W*. The letter *V* rarely doubles (*savvy*, *revved*, and the slang words *divvy* and *civvies* are exceptions).

V/CV (long)	VC/V (short)	VVCV (long)
human	**wagon**	**reason**
pilot	river	meeting
frozen	visit	peanut
student	never	leader
humor	planet	sneaker
lazy	lemon	easy
music	finish	
	seven	
	present	
	second	
	minute	

SORT 17   SYLLABLE JUNCTURE IN VCCCV AND VV PATTERNS

The VV juncture pattern represents a variation of the open syllable with a juncture between the two vowels. In these words the split can come after the first syllable, as in *cre-ate*, or after the second syllable as in *are-a*, but in either case there is an open syllable with the long-vowel sound. The VCCCV pattern is a variation of the closed syllable with the split between syllables coming before or after a consonant blend or digraph (*pil-grim*, *ath-lete*).

Introduce this sort with either a teacher-directed, guess my category, or student-centered sort. In a word hunt it will be hard for students to find many more VV words (*diary, radio, idea,* and *piano* are a few), but there are many VCCCV words that end in *-le* (*settle* for example). The study of words that end in *-le* is explored more in sorts 29 and 30, but would not be out of place here.

VCC/CV	VC/CCV	V/V
athlete	**pilgrim**	**create**
kingdom	complete	poet
pumpkin	monster	riot
halfway	kitchen	area
English	control	trial
mushroom	hundred	cruel
	inspect	lion
	children	diet
		idea
		video

SORT 18 OPEN AND CLOSED SYLLABLES AND INFLECTED ENDINGS

This extra sort is designed to help students see the relationship between the rules they learned for inflected endings and the syllable juncture patterns they have been studying in this unit. It reviews words from sorts 1–5 and does not need a full week of instruction unless you feel a thorough review of inflected endings is useful.

Put up the syllable juncture headings and ask students to sort the words as they have been doing for sorts 13–17. Ask them what they notice about the words in the first column. What rule did they learn about adding -ed and -ing to words like these? Repeat this with each column, helping students see how the rules for adding these inflected endings honor the syllable juncture patterns they have been studying. Pose questions such as: *If we did not double the p in hopping how would we be likely to read that word? (hoping) Why?* (The first syllable would look open since it would not clearly end with a consonant.) *Why don't we double the last letter in a word like acted?* (The syllable is already closed and ends with a consonant.) A second sort could be done under the headers of "e-drop," "double," and "nothing" to review the rules. In that sort *acted, wanted, standing,* and *hunted* would be separated from words that double.

VCV	VCCV	VVCV
hoping	**hopping**	**cleaning**
quoted	plotting	meeting
faded	spelling	waited
writing	nodded	shouting
skated	acted	floated
saving	wanted	needed
taking	standing	leaking
using	hunted	
	getting	

SPELL CHECK 2 ASSESSMENT FOR SYLLABLE JUNCTURE PATTERNS

Call out the words below for students to spell. All of these words have appeared in previous sorts.

1. summer
2. lion
3. reason
4. tiger
5. English
6. river
7. easy
8. moment
9. finish
10. hundred
11. video
12. number
13. poet
14. never
15. lazy
16. sister
17. leader
18. complete

To review all the syllable juncture patterns you may want to ask students to write the word in the appropriate category as shown below. Tell them to think about the letters in the middle of the words as you call them aloud. Then write each word under the heading that shows the pattern of letters in the middle. This form can be found on page 46 (Spell Check 2).

VCCV	VCCCV	VC/V first syllable short
summer	English	river
number	hundred	finish
sister	complete	never

V/CV first syllable long	VVCV	VV
tiger	reason	lion
moment	easy	video
lazy	leader	poet

VCV	VCCV	*oddball*
super	**supper**	diner
dinner	tiger	happy
later	busy	pretty
paper	penny	even
tiny	over	puppy
rabbit	ruler	kitten
hello	crazy	letter
lesson	summer	open

VCV	VCCV doublet	VCCV different	*oddball*
silent	**happen**		**basket**
matter	winter		follow
female	butter		problem
number	moment		pattern
sister	finger		bottom
chapter	fever		member
blanket	pillow		water
stupid	yellow		window

V/CV long	VC/V short	VVCV long
human	**wagon**	**reason**
river	pilot	visit
meeting	never	planet
lemon	frozen	peanut
finish	student	seven
leader	lazy	present
easy	second	music
sneaker	humor	minute

VCC/CV	VC/CCV	V/V
athlete	**pilgrim**	**create**
control	complete	children
poet	video	pumpkin
monster	riot	mushroom
halfway	kitchen	trial
area	English	hundred
cruel	idea	lion
kingdom	inspect	diet

VCV	VCCV	VVCV
hoping	hopping	cleaning
meeting	plotting	quoted
taking	spelling	waited
standing	getting	hunted
writing	nodded	shouting
skated	wanted	floated
leaking	using	needed
saving	acted	faded

Words Their Way: Word Sorts for Syllables and Affixes Spellers © 2005 by Prentice-Hall, Inc.

Spell Check #2 for Sorts 4–18

Name_____

Directions: Listen to the word you teacher calls aloud. Think of the letters in the middle of the word. Write the word under the heading that shows the pattern of letters.

1. **VCCV**	2. **VCCCV**	3. **VC/V** first syllable short

4. **V/CV** first syllable long	5. **VVCV**	6. **VV**

SORTS 19-30

Vowel Patterns in Accented Syllables

NOTES FOR THE TEACHER

The vowel patterns studied in the within word pattern stage reappear in two-syllable words in these sorts. For example, the *ai* pattern in *rain* is also in *painter* and *complain*. In these sorts students will revisit common vowel patterns and then less common vowel patterns. Because there are so many of these patterns this is a large unit containing 11 different sorts. It has been divided into two parts with a Spell Check following sort 23 to review the long-vowel patterns and a Spell Check following sort 30 to review the other vowel patterns. Students will also be introduced to the notion of accent or stress (we use these terms interchangeably) and helped to see that the vowel sound is clearly heard in the accented syllable. Sometimes students can "feel" the stress if they gently place the top of their hand under their chin as they say the words.

Note that stress may vary with regional dialects. Do you say *rac*coon or *raccoon*? Students may disagree at times about which syllable is stressed, and you may disagree with our categories as well. The dictionary can be consulted as the final arbiter. However, there is no reason to focus on right or wrong answers, and ambiguous words can simply go into the oddball category if desired. Many students will struggle to identify stressed syllables, but do not be overly concerned about this. Being able to identify the stressed syllable is not the primary goal in these sorts. Stress is simply one more way to understand the regularity of the spelling system and how vowel sounds and vowel patterns are fairly reliable in stressed syllables. Some understanding of syllable stress will also help students try alternative pronunciations when attempting to sound out an unfamiliar word or understand how to use the pronunciation guide for words they look up in the dictionary.

STANDARD WEEKLY ROUTINES FOR USE WITH SORTS 19-30

1. **Repeated Sorts, Writing Sorts, and Word Study Notebooks:** Students should sort their words independently and with a buddy (no-peeking or blind sorts) and record their sorts by writing them into columns. Challenge students to sort in different ways and record these different sorts in their word study notebooks.

2. **Break Words into Syllables and Indicate Accent:** Throughout this unit students will be thinking about where accent falls as well as how words are broken into syllables. They can be asked to indicate syllable division and syllable stress in their word study notebooks: _rain bow, a wake_. Students may not all agree with where stress falls, so do not be overly concerned about right and wrong answers. Once words are sorted by the syllable that contains the vowel pattern it is much easier to identify stressed syllables.

3. **Use the Dictionary:** Keep dictionaries handy and encourage their use when questions arise. Some of the words in these sorts and the ones to follow will not be as well known, and students should be encouraged to look up the meanings of words to add to the introductory discussion for each sort. Some suggestions are given in the sorts that follow about the use of the dictionary for specific features.

4. **Review Earlier Terms and Rules for Inflected Endings:** Students will see some familiar base words in many of these words (e.g., _painter, delight, lightning_). Point these out and talk about how they will be easier to spell when the base word is identified. Sometimes you may ask students to identify verbs and add -_ing_, -_ed_, or -_s_ to review the rules introduced in earlier sorts. You may also ask students to identify nouns and write the plural forms. These can be written in their word study notebooks. At other times you may review compound words or syllable juncture patterns.

5. **Word Hunts:** When students go on word hunts for vowel sounds welcome single-syllable words as well as two-syllable words since they will confirm that the same patterns are used to spell the sounds. Finding additional words with these same patterns may be challenging for students, so do not hold them accountable for finding any certain number of them in a word hunt. Instead you may want to focus on creating class lists that are added to throughout the unit.

6. **Games and Other Activities:** Games from _WTW_ that feature vowel patterns should work here. _Stressbusters_, a game described in Chapter 7, can be used throughout this unit with different words each week.

7. **Assessment:** To assess students' weekly mastery, ask them to spell the words in a standard spelling test format. You can also ask the students to set up their paper with headers and write the words under the correct column. It is not necessary to assess all 24 words. Students will need to be prepared to spell any of the words you select. A final spell check will assess retention of the words across the unit.

SORT 19   LONG -_A_ PATTERNS IN ACCENTED SYLLABLES

Demonstrate

Read the words aloud and discuss any that might be unfamiliar. Ask your students what they notice about this collection of words. They should notice that all the words have the long sound of _a_. Put up the two headers and key words. Point out that the long -_a_ sound is in the first syllable of _rainbow_ and in the second syllable of _awake_. Sort the rest of the words with the students' help. _Chocolate_ should go into the oddball column since it does not have the sound of long -_a_ even though the last syllable has the VCe pattern. When all the words have been sorted, read down each column, stressing the first syllable slightly. Explain to your students that the first syllable in each word is stressed or accented, and that when we say those words we put a little more emphasis on the first syllable. Have them read the words with you. Sometimes students can "feel" the stress if they gently place the top of their hand under their chin as they say the words. Repeat this with the second column where the stress is on the second syllable. The sort will look something like this:

1st	2nd	oddball
rainbow	**awake**	chocolate
painter	contain	
raisin	complain	
crayon	decay	
mayor	mistake	
maybe	parade	
bracelet	escape	
pavement	amaze	
basement	today	
payment	explain	
railroad	remain	
	obey	

During this same introductory lesson or on another day ask your students if they can think of another way to sort these words. Someone perhaps will mention the different patterns of long -*a*. Set up *rainbow*, *awake*, and *crayon* as headers and underline the spelling in each accented syllable. Sort the rest of the words with the students' help into one of these three categories. *Obey* will be an oddball since it has the sound of long -*a* but not one of the patterns. *Chocolate* has the pattern but not the sound. The sort will look something like the following:

r**ai**nbow	aw**a_ke_**	cra**y**on	oddball
painter	bracelet	mayor	obey
raisin	pavement	maybe	chocolate
contain	mistake	decay	
complain	parade	today	
railroad	amaze	payment	
explain	basement		
remain	escape		

Sort, Check, and Reflect

After modeling each sort have students repeat the sorts (both by syllable stress and vowel patterns) under your supervision. Have them check their sorts by looking for the pattern in each column. In these sorts students can tell where the accented syllable is by where the long -*a* pattern is. Encourage the students to reflect by asking them how the words in each column are alike and what they have learned.

Extend

Students should work with the words using some of the standard weekly routines. You may want to have students look up some of the words in a dictionary to see how accent or stress is indicated in the pronunciation guide. Dictionaries differ. Some may use accent marks and others use bold lettering. Students might then be asked to break their words into syllables and then indicate the accented syllables with an accent mark or by underlining. This can become a new routine to do throughout this unit in their word study notebooks. Ask students to add -*ing* and -*ed* to verbs such as *decay* (*decayed*, *decaying*), *escape* (*escaped*, *escaping*), *remain* (*remained*, *remaining*), and *explain* (*explained*, *explaining*).

SORT 20   LONG -*I* PATTERNS IN ACCENTED SYLLABLES

Introduce the sort in a manner similar to sort 19 above; that is, by the syllable containing the long -*i* sound. Sort the words a second time by the pattern for long -*i* using *frighten* and *polite* as headers. Underline the spelling of long -*i* to focus attention on the specific pattern. *Machine, forgive,* and *favorite* are oddballs that have familiar long -*i* patterns but do not have the long -*i* sound.

1st	2nd	oddball
frighten	**polite**	machine
ninety	delight	forgive
higher	surprise	favorite
driveway	decide	
slightly	advice	
lightning	survive	
sidewalk	combine	
highway	arrive	
brightly	provide	
	invite	
	describe	
	tonight	

Extend

Have students identify the compound words (*forgive, tonight, sidewalk, driveway, highway*) and then challenge them to find or think of other words that form compounds with *way* (*fairway, wayward, wayside,* etc.). Ask students to find words that contain a base word (e.g., *ninety*). Talk about the difference between compounds and base words (base words have an ending that cannot stand alone as a word).

SORT 21   LONG -O PATTERNS IN ACCENTED SYLLABLES

Introduce the sort in a manner similar to sort 19 above; that is, by the syllable containing the long -*o* sound. You may want to try a student-centered or guess my category sort as an alternative by removing the headers. Sort again by the patterns for long -*o* using *closely, hostess, owner* and *toaster* as headers. *Bureau* is an oddball that has the sound of long -*o* but not a familiar pattern. Consulting the dictionary will reveal several meanings for this word. Ask students to find three words that have the same base word (*lonely, lonesome,* and *alone*). Talk about how they are related in meaning.

Sort by Accented Syllable

1st	2nd	oddball
toaster	**below**	bureau
hostess	explode	Europe
lonely	suppose	
owner	compose	
lower	decode	
lonesome	remote	

loafer alone
closely approach
soapy awoke
bowling erode
poster
postage

Sort by Vowel Patterns

t**oa**ster	bel**ow**	expl**ode**	h**o**stess	*oddball*
loafer	owner	lonely	postage	bureau
soapy	lower	lonesome	poster	Europe
approach	bowling	closely		
		suppose		
		compose		
		decode		
		remote		
		alone		
		awoke		
		erode		

SORT 22   LONG -*U* PATTERNS IN ACCENTED SYLLABLES

Introduce the sort in a manner similar to sort 19 above; that is, by the syllable containing the long -*u* sound. You may want to try a student-centered or guess my category sort. Students will be familiar by now with the kinds of categories. *Produce* and *refuse* can be pronounced with the accent on the first syllable to indicate a different meaning (vegetables are *produce* and garbage is *refuse*), but the words are probably best known to students in elementary school as *refuse* and *produce*. These homographs are explored in sort 53. Sort again by the pattern for long -*u*. In a vowel pattern sort the following words will be oddballs: *Tuesday, beauty,* and *cougar*.

1st	2nd		Sort by Vowel Patterns		
rooster	**include**		r**oo**ster	incl**ude**	*oddball*
Tuesday*	refuse		moody	useful	Tuesday
useful	amuse		doodle	refuse	beauty
moody	confuse		toothache	amuse	cougar
doodle	perfume		noodle	confuse	
toothache	excuse		scooter	perfume	
noodle	pollute		balloon	excuse	
scooter	reduce		cartoon	pollute	
beauty*	balloon		raccoon	reduce	
cougar*	cartoon		shampoo	conclude	
	raccoon		cocoon		
	shampoo				
	cocoon				
	conclude				

* oddballs in pattern sort

SORT 23   LONG -E PATTERNS IN ACCENTED SYLLABLES

This sort is a little different because it includes the short sound of *e* (spelled *ea* as in *feather*) as well as the long sound. Ask students what they notice about the words for this week. There are many things they may say, such as that the words have both long and short -*e* sounds, which is different from the sorts they have been doing prior to this. Set up three headers and sort the words with the students' help, making sure that they attend to the sound of the vowel as well as to where the stressed pattern lies. Help students see that the same principles apply: In the stressed syllable we can clearly hear the vowel sound whether it is long or short. Sort again by both pattern and sound as shown in the second sort below.

Sort by Long or Short Sound in Accented Syllable

1st long	1st short	2nd long
needle	**feather**	**succeed**
season	leather	increase
reader	heavy	compete
feature	pleasant	defeat
freedom	sweater	indeed
meaning	steady	extreme
eastern	healthy	fifteen
people		thirteen
		repeat

Sort by Pattern and Sound

n**ee**dle	comp**ete**	s**ea**son	f**ea**ther	oddball
succeed	extreme	defeat	leather	people
fifteen		repeat	heavy	
thirteen		meaning	pleasant	
indeed		eastern	sweater	
freedom		reader	steady	
		increase	healthy	

SPELL CHECK 3 ASSESSMENT FOR LONG VOWEL PATTERNS IN ACCENTED SYLLABLES

Retention Test

The words below have been selected from previous lessons. (You may want to use different ones.) Call them aloud for students to spell on a sheet of notebook paper. You can also ask students to rewrite them into categories and explain why they grouped them together.

1. complain	7. highway	13. invite
2. soapy	8. awake	14. sweater
3. season	9. explode	15. poster
4. Tuesday	10. freedom	16. payment
5. fifteen	11. refuse	17. advice
6. owner	12. balloon	18. compete

SORT 24   AMBIGUOUS VOWELS – OY/OI AND OU/OW

Now we move into the study of vowels that are neither long nor short, or what we call ambiguous vowels in the context of syllable stress.

Demonstrate, Sort, Check and Reflect:

Begin by sorting words by accent using the headers **1**st and **2**nd to indicate which syllable is stressed. Then ask your students about the sound in the accented syllables under each header. Three different vowel sounds are included under the first header and two under the second. Set up these categories with the key words and then sort the rest of the words with student help as shown in the table below. A second sort by sound as well as pattern can follow on another day. Use the key words as headers and underline the vowel pattern. Send students on a word hunt to find more words that will fit into these categories. Welcome single-syllable words as well since they will confirm that the same patterns are showing up.

Accent and Sound Sort

1st			2nd	
voyage	**drowsy**	**country**	**destroy**	**announce**
moisture	county	trouble	appoint	allow
loyal	counter	double	avoid	about
poison	thousand	southern	annoy	around
noisy	coward		employ	amount

Pattern Sort

vo<u>y</u>age	**m<u>oi</u>sture**	**dr<u>ow</u>sy**	**ann<u>ou</u>nce**	**c<u>ou</u>ntry**
annoy	poison	allow	county	trouble
loyal	noisy	coward	counter	double
employ	appoint		thousand	southern
destroy	avoid		about	
			around	
			amount	

Extend

The game of *Oygo*, described in Chapter 7 of *WTW*, and its variation *Owgo* can be used to reinforce the spellings of these words.

SORT 25   MORE AMBIGUOUS VOWELS IN ACCENTED SYLLABLES (AU/AW/AL)

Begin by discussing any word meanings that you think your students might not know such as *gnawed, gawking,* or *flawless.* These words all share the same sound in the first accented syllable, so there is no sort by accent. Instead the headers call attention to the different patterns that spell the sound. Start the sort by asking students how the words are all alike. Introduce the headers and key words and sort the rest of the words with the students' help. *All right* is included because students often misspell this as *alright,* making it into a compound word when it should not be. *Laughed* has the *au* pattern but does not have the sound. Since these words are already sorted by pattern there is no second sort to do.

au	*aw*	*al*	oddball
saucer	**awful**	**also**	laughed
author	awkward	always	all right
August	lawyer	almost	
autumn	awesome	although	
laundry	gnawed	already	
caution	gawking		
faucet	flawless		
sausage			
auction			
haunted			

SORT 26   *R*-INFLUENCED *A* IN ACCENTED SYLLABLES

This sort reviews two sounds associated with *r*-influenced *a*. The sound in the first syllable of *airplane* and the second syllable of *compare* is sometimes referred to as long, whereas the vowel sound in the first syllable of *garden* is referred to as short. Begin this sort by asking students about any words whose meaning they might not know (*declare* or *despair* perhaps) and then ask how the words are all alike. This can be done as a student-centered sort by removing the headers before giving the students the words to sort. *Toward* is an oddball that anticipates the further study of words that begin with *w* in sort 28. These words can be sorted again by pattern focusing upon the *air* in *airplane* and the *are* in *compare*.

1ˢᵗ *ar*	1ˢᵗ long -*a*	2ⁿᵈ long -*a*	oddball
garden	**airplane**	**compare**	toward
market	parents	aware	
carpet	haircut	despair	
harvest	dairy	repair	
marble	barefoot	declare	
hardly	careful	beware	
partner	barely		
pardon	fairy		
barber			

Extend

Ask students to identify the compound words (*haircut, airplane, toward*) and challenge them to find more compounds for *air* (*airmail, airport, airwaves, airline, aircraft*), *hair* (*haircut, hairpin, hairbrush*), and *foot* (*football, footprint, footstep, barefoot*). Ask students if *carpet* is a compound word. Why or why not? Review adding *es* to *dairy* and *fairy* where the *y* is changed to *i* (*dairies, fairies*).

SORT 27   *R*-INFLUENCED *O* IN ACCENTED SYLLABLES

Some discussion of word meanings may be needed with terms such as *ashore* or *corncob*. In these words the *r*-influenced sound of /or/ is spelled two ways (*or* and *ore*). Sort these words according to whether the stressed /or/ sound is heard in the first or second syllable. A second sort of words can separate out the ones that are spelled with -*ore*. *Sorry* is an oddball that has the pattern but an unexpected sound. *Reward* anticipates the next sort. You might draw students' attention to the first sound in *chorus*, which has the sound of hard *c* rather than the more familiar /ch/. (During the derivational relations stage students will learn that this is a common correspondence in words that come from Greek.)

1st	2nd	oddball
morning	**report**	sorry
shorter	record	reward
order	perform	
forest	ashore	
corner	before	
normal	explore	
forty	ignore	
northern	adore	
border	inform	
forward		
corncob		
chorus		
florist		

SORT 28   WORDS WITH THE *W* OR /W/ SOUND BEFORE THE VOWEL

Like *r*, *w* (or *u* when it has the /w/ sound as in *quarter*) can influence the vowel. In these words the sound of *w* exerts an influence on the vowel that follows it, changing the *ar* in *warmth* to sound like /or/ and the *or* in *worker* to a sound like /ər/. What would normally be a short *-a* in a CVC word like *watch* is the broad *-a* sound. In these words the focus is only on the first syllable. Discuss the meanings of words such as *squabble* that might not be familiar to your students. Students should be able to sort these words with little direction, but do spend time reflecting on what the sorts reveal. Help the students form generalizations about how *w* works in these words. In word hunts they can look for other words that begin with *w* (such as *window* or *weekend*) in which the vowel after the *w* is not influenced by it. This will help them see that this influence is limited to words that begin with *wa* or *wo*. Help them recall the word *reward* from the last sort. Have them add this word to their word study notebook under other *war* words to see that it is no longer an oddball. Remember that students may not always agree about the exact sound in a word because of variations in dialect. This is especially true of *r*-influenced vowels, so be ready to accept these differences and let students sort by their own dialect.

war	wor	wa
warmth	**worker**	**watch**
wardrobe	worse	waffle
warning	world	wander
warden	worry	squat
warrior	worthy	squash
quarter	worship	squabble
quarrel	worthwhile	squad
swarm		
dwarf		
backward		

SORT 29   SCHWA + *R* SPELLED *ER*, *IR*, AND *UR* IN FIRST SYLLABLES

In these words the same *r*-influenced vowel sound in the first syllable is spelled three different ways, so you can introduce this sort in a manner similar to sort 25. *Spirit* and *merry* are oddballs because they have the spelling pattern, but not the sound of the words in this sort.

er	ir	ur	oddball
nervous	**thirty**	**sturdy**	spirit
person	firmly	purpose	merry
perfect	dirty	further	
certain	birthday	hurry	
mermaid	thirsty	purple	
perhaps	birdbath	turtle	
service		furnish	
		during	
		Thursday	

SORT 30   SCHWA + *R* AND *R*-INFLUENCED *E* IN ACCENTED SYLLABLES (*ER* / *EAR* / *ERE*)

This is a somewhat complicated sort that you should introduce as teacher-directed. Begin with just a sound sort using just two headers to represent the two sounds: *er* /ər/ and *ear/ere/eer* (r-influenced long -e). After sorting by the sound in the accented syllable ask your students what they notice about the spellings in each column (the ər sound is spelled with both *er* and *ear*). Use the key words to establish subcategories and sort the words by pattern so that the final sort looks something like the following:

schwa +r		r-influenced long -e		
er =/ur/	*ear* = /ur/	*ear/ere/eer*		
mercy	**early**	**nearby**	**severe**	**career**
sermon	earthquake	teardrop	sincere	cheerful
serpent	learner	spearmint	adhere	
hermit	pearly	yearbook	merely	
thermos	rehearse	appear		
kernel	yearn	dreary		

SPELL CHECK 4 ASSESSMENT FOR *R*-INFLUENCED AND AMBIGUOUS VOWELS IN ACCENTED SYLLABLES

Retention Test

The words below have been selected from previous lessons. (You may want to use different ones.) Call them aloud for students to spell on a sheet of notebook paper and then ask the students to rewrite them into categories and explain why they grouped them together.

1. noisy
2. autumn
3. marble
4. forest
5. quarter
6. person
7. nearby
8. thousand
9. before
10. awful
11. repair
12. amount
13. sincere
14. worry
15. thirty
16. early
17. Thursday
18. destroy
19. always
20. rarely

1st	2nd	*oddball*
rainbow	**awake**	painter
contain	obey	raisin
complain	decay	crayon
mistake	chocolate	parade
mayor	maybe	basement
escape	bracelet	amaze
railroad	today	pavement
explain	payment	remain

1st	2nd	*oddball*
frighten	**polite**	surprise
decide	advice	machine
survive	driveway	combine
forgive	provide	slightly
ninety	invite	favorite
describe	lightning	tonight
sidewalk	higher	brightly
delight	arrive	highway

Words Their Way: Word Sorts for Syllables and Affixes Spellers © 2005 by Prentice-Hall, Inc.

1st	2nd	*oddball*
toaster	**below**	closely
alone	hostess	explode
bureau	suppose	lonely
compose	owner	decode
lower	remote	lonesome
approach	loafer	awoke
postage	soapy	rowboat
bowling	erode	poster

1st	2nd	*oddball*
rooster	**include**	Tuesday
reduce	balloon	useful
cartoon	doodle	perfume
moody	refuse	raccoon
toothache	excuse	noodle
beauty	shampoo	pollute
conclude	scooter	confuse
cocoon	cougar	amuse

Words Their Way: Word Sorts for Syllables and Affixes Spellers © 2005 by Prentice-Hall, Inc.

1st long	1st short	2nd long
needle	feather	succeed
season	increase	leather
compete	repeat	defeat
feature	heavy	freedom
pleasant	meaning	indeed
extreme	fifteen	sweater
eastern	steady	healthy
people	reader	thirteen

1st	2nd	
voyage	**announce**	**drowsy**
destroy	**country**	moisture
coward	amount	thousand
avoid	poison	trouble
noisy	annoy	employ
allow	double	loyal
county	around	about
appoint	counter	southern

Words Their Way: Word Sorts for Syllables and Affixes Spellers © 2005 by Prentice-Hall, Inc.

au	*aw*	*al*
saucer	**awful**	**also**
always	author	almost
August	all right	lawyer
although	awkward	autumn
laundry	laughed	awesome
gnawed	caution	flawless
faucet	already	auction
gawking	sausage	haunted

1st *ar*	1st long -*a*	2nd long -*a*
garden	**airplane**	**compare**
careful	market	aware
carpet	despair	parents
toward	haircut	harvest
marble	repair	barefoot
fairy	hardly	declare
partner	beware	pardon
barber	barely	dairy

Words Their Way: Word Sorts for Syllables and Affixes Spellers © 2005 by Prentice-Hall, Inc.

1st	2nd	*oddball*
morning	**report**	order
record	shorter	perform
forest	sorry	normal
reward	corner	ashore
forty	before	northern
explore	border	forward
corncob	chorus	ignore
adore	florist	inform

war	*wor*	*wa*
warmth	**worker**	**watch**
quarter	wardrobe	worse
world	waffle	warden
warning	worry	squad
squat	warrior	worthy
quarrel	worship	swarm
worthwhile	dwarf	squabble
squash	wander	backward

Words Their Way: Word Sorts for Syllables and Affixes Spellers © 2005 by Prentice-Hall, Inc.

er	ir	ur	oddball
nervous	thirty	sturdy	
firmly	person	purpose	
perfect	further	dirty	
hurry	birthday	certain	
spirit	mermaid	Thursday	
perhaps	turtle	thirsty	
birdbath	service	furnish	
during	merry	purple	

Words Their Way: Word Sorts for Syllables and Affixes Spellers © 2005 by Prentice-Hall, Inc

er = /ur/	*ear* = /ur/	*ear* / *ere* / *eer*
mercy	**early**	**nearby**
career	**severe**	earthquake
spearmint	sermon	teardrop
kernel	pearly	yearbook
sincere	hermit	learner
rehearse	appear	thermos
adhere	dreary	cheerful
yearn	serpent	merely

SORTS 31–37

Unaccented Syllables

NOTES FOR THE TEACHER

In the previous sorts the feature of attention was familiar vowel patterns in the accented syllable. Now we turn our attention to the unaccented syllable in which the sound is often the *schwa* sound /ə/, as in the first syllable of *about*, or the final sound in *table* or *nickel*. These unaccented syllables are challenging to spell because the same sound is spelled several different ways (Is it *nickel*, *nickle*, or *nickil*?) and sound is not a useful clue. While there are some generalizations that govern which spelling is used, students must also memorize which spelling goes with a particular word, and repeated sorts will help them do this. As these sorts will show, however, some spellings are much more likely than others and this can lead to a "best guess" strategy. The ending *-le* is far more common than the endings *-el*, *-il*, *-or*, *-al*, and *-er* is much more common than *-or* or *-ar*. Students will also learn that the comparative adjective (*bigger*, *better*) is always spelled with *-er*.

STANDARD WEEKLY ROUTINES

1. **Repeated Work with the Words:** As usual, each student should get his or her own copy of words to cut apart for sorting, and you might want to enlarge the blackline masters before copying. Students should repeat the sort several times independently and with a buddy (no-peeking or blind sorts and writing sorts) after the sort has been modeled and discussed under the teacher's direction. See Chapter 3 in *WTW* for tips on managing sorting and homework routines.
2. **Writing Sorts and Word Study Notebooks:** Students should record their word sorts by writing them into columns in their notebooks or "Word Work at Home" sheets under the same key words that headed the columns of their word sort. At the bottom of the writing sort, have your students **reflect** on what they learned in that particular sort.
3. **Word Hunts:** Word hunts in daily reading materials will turn up additional words for most of these sorts and will help students develop a sense of the frequency of certain spellings. After they find examples they can add the words to the bottom of the proper column in their word study notebook. You may want to create class lists of all the words students find for each category to enhance these discoveries.
4. **Games and Other Activities:** Create games and activities such as those in *WTW*. The *Apple and Bushel Game* in Chapter 7 is appropriate and can be adapted for other unaccented syllables. *Dinosaur Take-a-Card* (for *-el*, *-le*, *-il*, and *-al*) and *Feed the Alligator* (for *-an*, *-in*, *-on*, and *-ain*) can be downloaded ready to use from the *WTWCD* and these games can also be adapted for other endings.

5. **Use the Dictionary:** Some of the words in these sorts may not be well known, so we urge you to discuss their meanings before introducing the sort. You may want students to look up the meanings of some words to add to the discussion.

6. **Assessment:** As usual, students can be assessed each week by asking them to spell the words they have worked with over the week. You may call out 10 or 15 words as a sample. A Spell Check for this unit can be found on page 75.

SORT 31   UNACCENTED FINAL SYLLABLE (-*LE*)

Demonstrate

Prepare a set of words to use for teacher-directed modeling. Write up the words *super*, *butter*, and *basket* and remind students of the syllable juncture patterns they assigned to these words: VCV, and VCCV (with and without doublets). Underline the corresponding letters in the words, as in the VCV pattern in *super*. Tell your students that they will be reviewing juncture patterns in the words for this week. Hand out or put on an overhead a copy of all the words and ask students what they notice about the words (e.g., all have two syllables, all end with -*le*). Go over any words students might not know. Put up the headers and key words (*title*, *little*, and *simple*) and point out the syllable juncture pattern that precedes the ending of -*le*. Explain to students that -*le* is always connected to a consonant and the syllable juncture patterns are modified to reflect this. For example VCV is now represented as VCle. Sort the rest of the words with the students' help.

Talk about how the words in each column are alike. Explain how the VCle pattern in *title* is divided after the vowel to make the open syllable (*ti-tle*) with a long-vowel sound, while the VCCle pattern in *little* and *simple* is divided between the consonants, resulting in closed syllables (*lit-tle* and *sim-ple*) with short vowels. Ask your students: *Which words will have open syllables with long-vowel sounds in the first syllable? Which words will have closed syllables with short-vowel sounds in the first syllable?*

Review accent or syllable stress by asking students what they notice when they read the columns of words. In these words the stress always falls on the first syllable, making the second and last syllables *unaccented*. Students might be directed to the dictionary to look up several words and see how the final syllable is represented in the pronunciation guide for the word. Explain that the upside-down *e* (ə) is called a *schwa* sound. (Note: Dictionaries differ. Check in advance to see how these sounds are represented.)

VCle	VCCle doublet	VCCle
title	**little**	**simple**
cradle	middle	tremble
able	settle	single
table	bottle	muscle
rifle	apple	sample
bridle	paddle	jungle
bugle	rattle	handle
cable	battle	candle

Sort, Check, and Reflect

After modeling the sort have students cut apart and shuffle their cards and sort them using the same headers and key words. After the students sort, have them check their own sorts by looking for the pattern in each column. If students don't notice a mistake, guide them to it by saying: *One of these doesn't fit. See if you can find it.* Encourage reflections by asking the students how the words in each column are alike and how they are different from the other words.

Extend

Word hunts will turn up lots of words that end in *-le*, including some that will have a different vowel pattern associated with a familiar syllable juncture pattern (such as *double*), which can go in an oddball category. See the list of standard weekly routines for follow-up activities to the basic sorting lesson.

SORT 32   UNACCENTED FINAL SYLLABLE (əL SPELLED *LE/EL/IL/AL*)

You may want to introduce this with a short spelling test. Ask students to spell *cattle*, *model, pencil,* and *final*. Talk about what makes the words hard to spell (they all have the same /əl/ sound in the final unaccented syllable). If you start with a student-directed sort cut off the headers before making copies. Hand out the words and go over any that students might not know. Ask the students what they notice about all the words and elicit ideas about how they might sort them. Students might suggest sorting by syllable juncture patterns as they did in the previous sort, or they might suggest sorting by the spelling in the final syllable as shown in the sort below. Read the columns of words to discover where the accent falls in the words. You may want to focus on the words *angle* and *angel* and speculate about why they are spelled as they are (the *g* in *angel* is "softened" by the following *e* but remains hard before the *l* in *angle*).

-le	*-el*	*-il*	*-al*	oddball
cattle	**model**	**pencil**	**final**	fragile
saddle	level	April	total	special
couple	angel	fossil	metal	
angle	novel	evil	signal	
	cancel		local	
	vowel		journal	
	jewel			
	towel			

Extend

A word hunt will be very useful with this sort. Although the *-le* column is quite short here, it is by far the most common spelling and will turn up in word hunts with the greatest frequency. Words spelled with *-el* are not too rare, but students will find it challenging to find more words for the *-il* and *-al* categories. At some point compile a list of all the words students have found, including the words from last week, and talk about the relative frequencies of each. Ask students to form a "best guess" strategy if they hear the sound in a word that they are not sure how to spell. How would they spell the name *Mable*? Or the word *frindle*? (*Frindle* is the name of a book by Andrew Clements in which a boy decides to invent a new word and, of course, has to invent a spelling for it also.) The *Apple and Bushel Game*, described in Chapter 7 of *WTW*, is designed to differentiate between *-el* and *-le* endings and can be adapted to include *-il* and *-al* as well. The game of *Dinosaur Take-a-Card*, available on the *WTWCD*, reviews all four.

SORT 33   FINAL UNACCENTED SYLLABLE (ǝR/ SPELLED ER/AR/OR)

You might begin this sort with a short spelling test in which you ask students to spell three words: *cover, doctor,* and *collar.* As in previous sorts, compare their spellings as a way to highlight the problem spellers face when they can hear the sound in the final unaccented syllable but are not sure how to spell it. Show students the words for this week and read them aloud. Talk about how the final sound is exactly the same but has several spellings. Ask them to hypothesize about which one is most common. Proceed with a teacher-directed or student-centered sort that will look something like the sort below. Again, review the idea of accent or stress by reading the columns of words to find that the final syllable in these words (e.g., words ending in /el/) is unaccented. Again, have students use the dictionary to check how the unaccented syllable is represented in the pronunciation guide.

-er	*-or*	*-ar*
spider	**color**	**collar**
brother	doctor	dollar
rather	favor	solar
cover	flavor	sugar
silver	mirror	grammar
weather	motor	
father	rumor	
flower	tractor	
mother	harbor	
after		

Extend

As described for sort 32 earlier, use a word hunt to answer the question of frequency and compile a master list of all the words students can find. You can also challenge students to sort the words they find by parts of speech. They will find many adjectives and nouns that will anticipate the sort for next week.

SORT 34   AGENTS AND COMPARATIVES

You might begin the study of agents (i.e., people who do things) and comparatives by looking at the master word hunt list. Ask students to find words that name people who do things (agents). Ask them if there is another category of words they can find. Prompt them by asking how words like *bigger* and *older* (select comparative words from your list) are alike. Explain that these words can be called *comparative adjectives.* Begin this two-step sort by using the headers and sorting all the words into two categories. Then pull out the key words to head up subcategories and sort the words further by the spelling of the final unaccented syllable.

People who do things			Words to compare
dancer	**actor**	**beggar**	**bigger**
dreamer	creator	burglar	sooner
driver	sailor		better
farmer	visitor		smaller
jogger	editor		fresher
writer			younger
stranger			older
swimmer			smoother
voter			

Extend

Write up the word *beg, begging, begged,* and *beggar.* Ask students what they notice about the spelling and review with them the rules they learned about adding *-ed* and *-ing* to words with VC at the end. Explain that similar rules ("double, *e*-drop, and nothing") apply when adding these endings to a word. Repeat with *drive, driving,* and *driver.* Ask the students to sort the words for this week (that have base words) according to the rule that applies to the base word, as shown below. Have them add this sort to their word study notebook. On the weekly assessment check for transfer by asking students to spell *shopper, diver,* and *catcher.*

double	e-drop	nothing	oddball
beggar	driver	dreamer	editor *
jogger	writer	farmer	visitor *
swimmer	stranger	sailor	
bigger	voter	sooner	
	creator	smaller	
	dancer	younger	
		older	
		smoother	

Note: better *and* burglar *don't have base words that are related in meaning.*

*editor *and* visitor *actually follow the more advanced inflection rule, which states that the final consonant will double only if it is in the accented syllable. Hence* admitting *doubles, but* editing *does not.*

SORT 35   MORE FINAL *R* SPELLINGS (/CHəR/ZHəR/YəR/)

The unaccented final syllables in these words have two spellings (*-er* and *-ure*) and several sounds (/chur/, /zhur/, and /yur/) that are similar but subtly different. While we ask students to sort by the sounds do not be overly concerned if there is disagreement and inconsistency. The point is not as much to sort the words correctly by sound as it is to see that the words are spelled with the same pattern (*-ure*) despite these slight differences. Since this is a more challenging sort, model it in a teacher-directed sort. Put up the headers and a key word for each. Explain that the slash marks indicate a sound that goes with the spelling pattern above and pronounce them for the students. Say each key word and stress the sound in the final syllable. Sort the rest of the words, taking the time to say each word, and have the students repeat it and then compare it to the key words or headers before sorting. *Senior* and *danger* are oddballs that have similar sounds but different spellings.

-cher = /chur/	-ture = /chur/	-sure = /zhur/	-ure = /yur/	oddball
catcher	**picture**	**measure**	**figure**	senior
rancher	nature	pressure*	failure	danger
teacher	capture	pleasure		
pitcher	future	leisure		
	mixture	treasure		
	creature			
	pasture			
	posture			
	torture			
	culture			
	injure			

*might be closer to /shur/ than /zhur/ to some ears

Extend

The game *You're Up* in Chapter 7 of *WTW* is designed to reinforce the spelling of these words.

SORT 36   FINAL /əN/ SPELLED *EN, ON, IN,* AND *AIN*

Students should be able to do this as an open sort using the spelling patterns in the final syllable. Use word hunts to determine the "best guess" strategy based on frequency.

-en	*-on*	*-ain*	*-in*	oddball
broken	**dragon**	**mountain**	**cousin**	mission
eleven	cotton	captain	cabin	
hidden	gallon	bargain	napkin	
heaven	ribbon	fountain	penguin	
chosen	apron	curtain	violin	
stolen	bacon			
mitten				

Extend

See the game *Feed the Alligator* on the *WTWCD*.

SORT 37   UNACCENTED INITIAL SYLLABLES (*A-, DE-, BE-*)

In these words the first syllable is unaccented and has the schwa sound (ə-gain, də-bate, bə-yond). Some of these words (*again, among, awhile, because, before, belong*) appeared in a within word pattern sort but are revisited here. Many rank as "spelling demons" that students struggle to spell across the grades. As in final unaccented syllables, students should be led to see that sound cannot always be trusted as a guide to spelling the unaccented syllable in these words. Nevertheless, the words fall into categories that share similar spelling patterns. Expect some lively debate about the exact pronunciation of some of these words. We sometimes stress a different syllable when we say a word in isolation or when we are thinking about the spelling. For example we might say *beyond* with a long *-e* vowel sound at times, but when we use it in a sentence we probably say /bə-yond/. Stressing normally unaccented syllables is actually a good spelling strategy that works well with words like these and you might suggest that to your students. Although we may disagree about the exact sound and syllable stress, the spelling patterns can clearly be sorted as shown below. The oddballs include a few words that have the unaccented sound in the first syllable but a different spelling pattern. You might begin with a sound sort and then look for words that do not fit the patterns to find the oddballs.

a-	*de-*	*be-*	oddball
again	**debate**	**beyond**	divide
another	degree	believe	direct
awhile	depend	between	upon
among	desire	beneath	
aboard	develop	because	
against	defend	begun	
afraid			
aloud			
agreed			

SPELL CHECK 5 ASSESSMENT FOR UNACCENTED SYLLABLES

Retention Test

The words below have been selected from previous lessons. (You may want to use different ones.) Call them aloud for students to spell on a sheet of notebook paper. You can also ask students to rewrite them into categories and explain why they grouped them together.

1. visitor
2. brother
3. capture
4. model
5. gallon
6. afraid
7. favor
8. measure
9. title
10. eleven
11. April
12. younger
13. signal
14. dollar
15. degree
16. middle
17. napkin
18. because

VCle	VCCle doublet	VCCle
title	**little**	**simple**
middle	able	tremble
cable	single	settle
bottle	table	muscle
cradle	apple	paddle
rattle	jungle	bridle
bugle	battle	handle
candle	sample	rifle

Words Their Way: Word Sorts for Syllables and Affixes Spellers © 2005 by Prentice-Hall, Inc.

-*le*	-*el*	-*al*	-*il*
cattle	model	final	
pencil	level	April	
total	saddle	angel	
novel	fossil	metal	
couple	cancel	fragile	
jewel	special	vowel	
signal	journal	angle	
evil	towel	local	

-er	-or	-ar
spider	color	collar
doctor	brother	sugar
rather	dollar	favor
solar	cover	silver
weather	flavor	mother
flower	father	mirror
after	rumor	motor
tractor	grammar	harbor

Words Their Way: Word Sorts for Syllables and Affixes Spellers © 2005 by Prentice-Hall, Inc.

People who do things	Words used to compare	
dancer	bigger	actor
beggar	dreamer	sooner
better	smaller	driver
farmer	burglar	creator
fresher	jogger	younger
writer	older	sailor
smoother	swimmer	visitor
editor	stranger	voter

-*cher* = /chur/	-*ture* = /chur/	-*sure* = /zhur/	-*ure* = /yur/
catcher		picture	measure
figure	danger		failure
pressure	rancher		capture
future	figure		treasure
teacher	mixture		senior
pleasure	creature		culture
pasture	leisure		pitcher
injure	torture		posture

-en	*-on*	*-ain*	*-in*
broken	**dragon**	**mountain**	
cousin	eleven	cotton	
gallon	captain	hidden	
heaven	cabin	ribbon	
bargain	chosen	napkin	
mission	apron	fountain	
stolen	bacon	mitten	
violin	curtain	penguin	

a-	de-	be-	oddball
again	**debate**		**beyond**
degree	another		believe
divide	depend		awhile
among	between		desire
develop	aboard		upon
against	beneath		afraid
because	aloud		defend
agreed	begun		direct

SORTS 38-44

Exploring Consonants

NOTES FOR THE TEACHER

Consonants continue to be explored at all levels of spelling. Hard and soft *g* and *c* were introduced in the within word pattern stage but are revisited here at the beginning and end of longer words. Whether the sound of *g* or *c* is hard or soft depends on the vowel that follows it, and this can account for some interesting spellings. Sort 38 looks at initial hard and soft *g* and *c*. This sort lays the foundation for sorts 39 and 40, where hard and soft generalizations apply to words that end in *-ge* and *-ce*, and explains why there is a place holder (the letter *u*) between *g* and *i* in the word *guide* and between *g* and *e* in the word *tongue*. Without the *u* the sound of *g* would become soft (/jide/ or /tonj/).

The spelling of the /k/ sound in English is not as simple as most consonant sounds in words of more than one syllable. Although students learned the final *ck* in relation to short vowels in the within word pattern stage, *ck* is revisited here in the middle of two-syllable words. Other /k/ spellings, such as *ic*, *x*, and *que*, are also explored in sorts 41 and 42.

Words with silent letters at the beginning (*honest*, *knuckle*) and in the middle of words (*listen*, *thought*) are examined in sort 43. *Ph* consistently spells the sound of /f/, usually in words that derive from Greek. *Gh* is often silent but can also represent the sound of /f/ at the end of some words. Some more advanced vocabulary that foreshadows the study of Greek combining forms in derivational relations will be covered in sort 44.

STANDARD WEEKLY ROUTINES

1. **Repeated Work, Word Study Notebooks, and Word Hunts:** Students should repeat the sort several times independently and with a buddy (no-peeking or blind sorts and writing sorts) after the sort has been modeled and discussed under the teacher's direction. Students should record their word sorts by writing them and reflect on what they learned in that particular sort. Word hunts in daily reading materials will turn up additional words for most of these sorts.

2. **Use the Dictionary:** Some of the words in these sorts may not be well known, so you should discuss these before introducing the sort. Students should be encouraged to look up some meanings of words to add to the discussion. A few words might also be assigned to look up for a word study notebook activity.

3. **Assessment:** As usual, students can be assessed each week by asking them to spell the words they have worked with over the week. You could call out only 10 or 15 words as a sample. A Spell Check for this unit can be found on page 88.

SORT 38   HARD AND SOFT *G* AND *C*

Demonstrate

This sort has several steps, so allow some extra time, or do it over several days. Read over the words and talk about any that might be unfamiliar. Begin by sorting the words into two columns by the beginning letter (*g* or *c*). Then read all the words in the *c* column and ask students what they notice about the sound spelled with *c* at the beginning (sometimes it sounds like /k/ and sometimes like /s/). Explain that these sounds are called **hard** *c* and **soft** *c* and introduce the headers. Repeat with the other words beginning with *g*. The sort will look something like the following:

Sort by Initial Sounds

Soft *c*	Soft *g*	Hard *c*	Hard *g*
cement	**gentle**	**correct**	**gather**
circle	gymnast	common	gossip
central	giraffe	contest	golden
century	genius	college	garage
cyclist	general	custom	gutter
cider	gingerbread	collect	
cereal			

Next, combine all the soft *g* and soft *c* words. Ask students if they notice anything about the vowel in these words. Repeat this with the hard *c* and hard *g* words. Suggest that they try sorting the words by the second letter in each word. The final sort will reveal that the hard and soft sounds are related to the vowel that follows. Underline the vowel that follows the *c* or *g* as a key word for each column. This sort will look something like the following:

Sort by Vowel that Follows the Initial Letter

Soft *g* and Soft *c*			Hard *g* and Hard *c*		
c<u>e</u>ment	c<u>i</u>rcle	c<u>y</u>clist	g<u>a</u>ther	c<u>o</u>rrect	c<u>u</u>stom
central	cider	gymnast	garage	common	gutter
century	giraffe				contest
cereal					college
gentle					collect
genius					gossip
general					golden
gingerbread					

Sort, Check, and Reflect

After modeling the sort have students cut apart and sort their own words into both sorts. You might have them underline the vowel to create headers for the second sort as shown above and to check after sorting. Encourage reflections by asking the students how the words in each column are alike and how they are different from the other words. Help students formulate a generalization that goes something like this: *c* and *g* are usually soft when followed by *e*, *i*, or *y* and hard when followed by *a*, *o*, or *u*.

Extend

Students should repeat these sorts several times and record them in their word study notebook. See the list of standard weekly routines for follow-up activities to the basic sorting lesson. Word hunts may not turn up many more words but some include: *gesture, goblin, gobble, goggles, guppy,* and *gerbil. Giant, center, circus, ginger,* and *cycle* were included in the within word pattern sort for hard and soft *g* and *c* Accept one-syllable words, such as *camp* and *goat,* and expect some oddballs, such as *girl* and *gift.*

SORT 39   S AND SOFT C AND G IN THE FINAL SYLLABLE
Demonstrate, Sort, Check, and Reflect

Go over the words to read them and discuss their meanings. Remind students that in the previous sort they looked at the sounds of hard and soft *g* at the beginnings of words. Explain that now they will examine soft *g* (/j/) and *c* (/s/) at the ends of words. Ask them what they notice about the words in this sort. Talk about possible headers and then sort the words, starting with the key words. Remind students that letters inside slanted lines, /j/ for example, represent a sound. Talk about how words in each column are alike by sound and the spelling pattern used to spell the sound. *Surgeon* might be an oddball or go under the *-ge-* pattern. Talk about how *surgeon* would have to be pronounced if the *e* were dropped: /surgon/. Do the same thing with words under *-ce*. If the *e* were dropped in the word *notice* we would probably want to say /notick/. Repeat with other words to help students reflect on why these words have an *e* after the *c* or *g*. Help students form a generalization such as the following: At the end of words the final sound of /s/ can be spelled *-ce* or *-ss* and the soft sound of *g* is often followed by the letter *e*.

ce = /s/	*ss* = /s/	*-ge-* = /j/	*age* = /ij/
notice	**recess**	**budget**	**bandage**
police	princess	midget	garbage
sentence	actress	gadget	manage
distance	address	surgeon*	luggage
office	compass		package
science			village
practice			message
			courage

Surgeon may be sorted as an oddball.

Extend

Review plurals by asking students to add *-s* or *-es* to these words from the sort: *princess, actress, address.* Review the final sound in *voyage* and *garage* from earlier sorts.

SORT 40   MORE WORDS WITH G
Demonstrate, Sort, Check, and Reflect

Introduce this sort in a manner similar to sort 39. In these words the sound of *g* is always hard because it is followed by a placeholder, the silent letter *u*, to separate it from a vowel that would otherwise make it soft. *Guard* is somewhat of an oddball because it really does not need the *u* to keep the *g* hard before the letter *a*. The other oddballs offer a chance to talk about the sound of *g* in each one. In *gauge* there is both a hard and a soft *g*, but no apparent reason for the *u*. In *language* the final *-age* is similar to words from the previous sort, but the *u* takes on a /w/ sound as it does in *penguin* from sort 34. In *argue* the *u* represents the long sound as well as keeping the *g* hard. Help students reflect on these words and form a generalization such as the following: Silent *u* is sometimes used to keep the *g* hard before *e* and *i*.

gu-	*-gue*	*-g*	oddball
guess	**tongue**	**ladybug**	gauge
guard	vague	zigzag	language
guitar	league	shrug	argue
guide	fatigue	iceberg	
guilty	catalogue*	strong	
guest	dialogue*		
guidance	plague		
	intrigue		
	synagogue		

catalog and *dialog* are alternative spellings for these words.

Extend

Word hunts may not be very productive with these spellings but might turn up *morgue, rogue, vogue, prologue,* and *mustang.* Have students look up *catalogue* and *dialogue* in the dictionary to see if there are alternative spellings for these words. Challenge students to think of other words besides *penguin* and *language* in which *gu* stands for a blend (/gw/). Words of Spanish origin such as *guacamole, iguana, saguaro, guava,* and *guano* have this sound and spelling. Spanish-speaking students might supply more Spanish words with the *gu* spelling. *Anguish* and *languish* have the sound as well.

SORT 41   THE SOUND OF *K* SPELLED *CK, IC,* AND *X*

Introduce this sort in a manner similar to the other sorts in this unit, noting how the /k/ sound (or /ks/ in the case of *x*) in the middle and end of these words is spelled with *ck, ic,* and *x. Stomach* is an oddball because it ends in a sound like /ick/ but is spelled in an unusual way. A word hunt will turn up many one-syllable words that end in *k* and may help students conclude that while one-syllable words that end in the /k/ sound are always spelled with -*k* (*leak*) or -*ck* (*lack*), most two-syllable words end in -*ic* except for compound words like *homesick.*

-ck	*ck*	*-ic*	*-x*	oddball
shock	**chicken**	**magic**	**relax**	stomach
quick	pocket	attic	index	
hammock	nickel	traffic	perplex	
attack	pickle	topic	complex	
	buckle	picnic		
	ticket	metric		
		electric		
		fabric		
		plastic		

Extend

The game of *Double Crazy Eights,* described in Chapter 7 of *WTW,* is designed to review the *k* and *ck* spellings and also reviews the rules of adding inflected endings to such words. When adding *ing* or *ed* to *picnic,* a final *k* must be added to keep the *c* from being "softened."

SORT 42   SPELLINGS WITH *QU*

Introduce this sort by asking how the words are all alike and talk about possible ways to sort them. The letters *q* and *u* together spell the /qw/ blend that can come in the first or second syllable of these words. *Qu* occasionally spells just the sound of /k/, as it does in the last column of words. Point out that *racquet* has a homophone spelled *racket* and talk about what both the words mean. There are not too many more words that students are likely to find in a word hunt (*mosque* is one) except one-syllable words such as *quit*.

1ˢᵗ syllable	2ⁿᵈ syllable	qu = /k/
question	**equal**	**antique**
quality	frequent	racquet
squirrel	equipment	mosquito
squirm	equator	conquer
quaint	equip	
quotation	banquet	
quizzes	inquire	
queasy	liquid	
	require	
	sequence	
	sequel	
	request	

SORT 43   WORDS WITH SILENT CONSONANTS

Go over these words to talk about the meaning of any that are unfamiliar. Ask students to figure out how these words are all alike (each one has a silent consonant). Introduce the headers and key words or let students establish the categories. The word *wrestle* has two silent letters and can go in two categories. Students should be challenged to find more words with silent consonants, and their search may turn up many familiar one-syllable words like *write*, *light*, and *knife*.

Silent *t*	Silent *g*	Silent *w*	Silent *k*	Silent *h*	Silent *gh*
castle	**design**	**wrinkle**	**knuckle**	**honest**	**through**
whistle	resign	wreckage	knowledge	honor	thought
fasten	assignment	wrestle		rhyme	brought
listen		answer		rhythm	bought
often					though
soften					
(wrestle)					

SORT 44   *GH* AND *PH*

Discuss the meaning of any words that might be unfamiliar to students such as *phantom*. Introduce this sort in a manner similar to the other sorts in this unit, noting how *ph* and *gh* represent /f/ and how *gh* is often silent in the middle of words. Remind students of the words from last week that had silent *gh* (*through*, *thought*, etc.). More of these high-frequency spelling demons are revisited this week.

ph-	*ph*	*-gh = /f/*	silent *gh*
phrase	**alphabet**	**enough**	**daughter**
physics	dolphin	cough	naughty
phantom	elephant	tough	taught
photocopy	nephew	rough	caught
photograph	orphan	laughter	fought
	trophy		
	telephone		
	homophone		
	paragraph		

SPELL CHECK 6 ASSESSMENT FOR CONSONANTS

Retention Test

The words below have been selected from previous lessons. (You may want to use different ones.) Call them aloud for students to spell on a sheet of notebook paper. You can then ask your students to rewrite them into categories and explain why they grouped them together.

1. central	8. contest	15. liquid
2. gossip	9. genius	16. thought
3. attack	10. ticket	17. trophy
4. sentence	11. village	18. address
5. plastic	12. guilty	19. vague
6. equal	13. index	20. enough
7. listen	14. answer	

Soft *c*	Hard *c*	Soft *g*	Hard *g*
cement	gentle		correct
gather	circle		common
gossip	gutter		golden
central	contest		college
giraffe	garage		century
custom	cereal		genius
cider	general		collect
gingerbread	gymnast		cyclist

ce = /s/	ss = /s/	ge = /j/	age = /ij/

notice	recess	budget
bandage	police	princess
midget	garbage	sentence
science	actress	manage
luggage	office	gadget
address	message	practice
package	compass	village
distance	surgeon	courage

Words Their Way: Word Sorts for Syllables and Affixes Spellers © 2005 by Prentice-Hall, Inc.

gu-	-gue	-g	oddball
guess	**tongue**		**ladybug**
gauge	zigzag		vague
league	guard		shrug
fatigue	iceberg		catalogue
guitar	language		guide
guilty	plague		intrigue
argue	guest		strong
guidance	dialogue		synagogue

-ck	-ck-	-ic	-x
shock	**chicken**		**magic**
relax	quick		pocket
attic	nickel		traffic
complex	topic		stomach
pickle	picnic		attack
metric	buckle		index
fabric	electric		ticket
hammock	plastic		perplex

Words Their Way: Word Sorts for Syllables and Affixes Spellers © 2005 by Prentice-Hall, Inc.

1st	2nd	*qu* = /k/
question	**equal**	**antique**
frequent	quality	equip
squirrel	liquid	racquet
require	squirm	inquire
quaint	equator	sequence
sequel	quotation	conquer
quizzes	banquet	request
equipment	mosquito	queasy

Words Their Way: Word Sorts for Syllables and Affixes Spellers © 2005 by Prentice-Hall, Inc.

silent t	silent g	silent w	silent k	silent h	silent gh
castle		design		wrinkle	
honest		through		knuckle	
bought		whistle		honor	
fasten		resign		wrestle	
rhyme		listen		thought	
often		brought		knowledge	
wreckage		soften		rhythm	
assignment		though		answer	

Words Their Way: Word Sorts for Syllables and Affixes Spellers © 2005 by Prentice-Hall, Inc.

ph-	*-ph-*	*gh* = /f/	silent *gh*
phrase	**alphabet**		**enough**
daughter	physics		dolphin
elephant	cough		nephew
tough	phantom		naughty
orphan	laughter		trophy
photocopy	telephone		taught
caught	paragraph		fought
photograph	homophone		rough

SORTS 45–51

Affixes

NOTES FOR THE TEACHER

The term "affixes" includes prefixes and suffixes and both will be introduced as meaning units (or morphemes) in these seven sorts. Unlike the inflected suffixes studied earlier, the affixes in these sorts change the meaning of the word (*lock* becomes the opposite *unlock)* or the part of speech (the verb *love* becomes the adjective *lovely* or *loveable*). The suffix *-er*, which can indicate agents and comparatives, has already been introduced although it was not identified as a suffix at the time. It will be revisited in sort 40 where it is added to words that end in *y*.

In these sorts much more attention will be paid to the meaning of the words **after** they are sorted rather than before, so we suggest you skip the usual practice of reading and discussing the meanings of unfamiliar words as the first step. These sorts foreshadow the derivational relations stage where meaning and the learning of new vocabulary take on greater importance in word study activities. The words in these sorts, however, are likely to be words that are known to most students (especially the base words) and the focus is upon learning about base words and affixes as meaning units that can be combined in many different ways. Often the spelling of these words is not especially challenging (*refill, unfair,* or even *carelessness*), being made up of base words that are very familiar and affixes that are spelled regularly. However, working with the sorts helps students see words and think of words as being made up of "chunks" or word parts that share meanings and spelling patterns.

Since suffixes change the base words' part of speech (e.g., *care* (a verb) becomes *careless* or *careful* (adjectives) and *carefully* (an adverb)), this is a good time to introduce or review parts of speech as part of your general language arts program. Students can sort words by their part of speech as an extension to the other sorts.

In several of these sorts students will be asked to recall and extend their knowledge of the rules covered earlier under inflected endings. They will find that the "double, drop, or nothing" and the "change *y* to *i*" rules will come into play when *-y, -ly, -er,* and *-est* are added to base words.

The study of prefixes in the upper grades is a good time to introduce dictionaries that have information about the origins of words. Interesting discoveries about base words and roots can be made, such as the relationship between using dental floss and indenting paragraphs (see sort 47). We encourage you to have at least one dictionary available with derivational information in the classroom and many online dictionaries will have this information as well. One source is *The American Heritage Dictionary* at **http://www.yourdictionary.com**.

STANDARD WEEKLY ROUTINES FOR USE WITH SORTS 45–51

1. **Repeated Sorts, Writing Sorts, and Word Study Notebooks:** Students should sort their words independently and with a buddy (no-peeking or blind sorts) and record their sorts by writing them into columns in their notebooks or on the "Word Work at Home" sheet in the appendix. Some specific suggestions are given for some activities in the sorts that follow.
2. **Word Hunts:** Students will find many more words in their daily reading that mirror the featured prefixes and suffixes and these can be added to the bottom of the proper column in their word study notebooks. Students may discover that dictionaries are a good place to find words with prefixes.
3. **Use Words in Sentences:** Students may not know the meaning of all these words, but meaning and use will be explored through the discussion and sorting. You may want to assign students a small number of sentences to write in their word study notebooks to help establish the meaning and use of the words.
4. **Use the Dictionary:** Ask students to look up the meanings of words to add to the discussion of prefixes and to resolve any questions about the meanings and origins of words.
5. **Games and Other Activities:** Games from *WTW* that work well for the features explored in this unit include *Jeopardy* and *Scattergories* in Chapter 7. The game of *Match*, described in Chapter 5, can be adapted for affixes.
6. **Assessment:** To assess students' weekly mastery, ask them to spell the words in a standard spelling test format. Remember that it is not necessary to assess all 24 words. Students will need to be prepared to spell any of the words you select. A final spell check will assess the students' retention of the words in all seven sorts as well as their ability to transfer their knowledge of how the base word sometimes changes when suffixes are added.

SORT 45   PREFIXES (*RE-* AND *UN-*)

Demonstrate

Prepare a set of words to use for teacher-directed modeling. Save the discussion of word meanings until after sorting. Display a transparency of the words on the overhead or hand out the sheet of words to the students. Ask them what they notice about the words and get ideas about how the words can be sorted. Students might note that the words all contain smaller words; remind them of the term **base words** that was used in the study of inflected endings. Put up the headers and key words and then sort the rest of the words. During this first sort the oddballs *uncle* and *reptile* might be included under *re-* and *un-*. They are there to help students see that these letters do not always spell a meaningful prefix added to a meaningful base word. Praise students if they notice this on the first sort!

The discussion after the first sort might go something like this: *Look at the words under* re-. *What do you notice about the meanings of these words?* Focus on the key word *rebuild*. Ask students for the base word. Explain that a **prefix** has been added to the base word and that it changes the meaning of the word. Ask students what *rebuild* means (to build something over again as in *We had to rebuild the barn after the tornado hit*). Repeat this with the other words under *re-*, talking about the meaning of each word: *Recopy* means to copy again; *recycle* means to use something again, and so on. The word *reptile* does not mean to do something again and should be transferred to the oddballs. Then explain that a prefix has a meaning of its own and ask the students what *re-* means in all the words (it means to do something again). Repeat this with the words under *un-* to determine that the prefix means "not" in words such as *unable* or *unselfish* but something more like "the opposite of" in words like *unwrap* and *unpack*. *Uncle* will be moved to the oddballs since it does not have a base word and does not mean the opposite of anything. Students might be asked to write the meaning of the prefix on the headers (e.g., *re-* = again).

re-	*un-*	oddball
rebuild	**unable**	uncle
recopy	unbeaten	reptile
recycle	unwrap	
refill	unselfish	
refinish	unbutton	
remodel	unkind	
retrace	unpack	
retake	unfair	
return	uneven	
review	unequal	
rewrite	unhappy	

Sort, Check, and Reflect

Students should repeat this sort several times and work with the words using some of the weekly routines listed above. When students write these words in their word study notebooks they might be asked to underline the prefix in each one and write the meaning of the prefix.

Extend

Word hunts will turn up lots of words that begin with *re-* and *un-*, including more oddballs such as *rescue*, which look like they might have a prefix until the meaning and base word are considered (sometimes these words are called false prefixes). Word hunts will also reveal other subtle variations in meaning for the prefix *re-* as well as words with no clear base words. Some words suggest the meaning "back" or "against" as in *restore, retort, reimburse, refund, rebound, rebate,* and *rebel*. If you have dictionaries available that give information about the origins of words, students can be asked to look up any words that they don't know the meaning of or that they have questions about. For example the word *rebel* does not have a familiar base word that stands alone, but a root word that comes from the Latin word *bellum*. How far you want to go with this is up to you and the level of understanding your students are ready to handle. Roots as word parts that come from Greek and Latin and do not stand alone as base words are explored thoroughly in the derivational relations stage.

SORT 46   PREFIXES (*DIS-, MIS-,* AND *PRE-*)

Begin this sort by asking students how to spell the word *misspell* (a word that is often misspelled). Have them speculate about why there are two *s*'s in the word, but do not offer an explanation yourself. Continue with this sort in a manner similar to sort 45; that is, sorting by the prefixes and then discussing the shared meanings of the words in each column. Help students discover that *dis-* means "the opposite of," *mis-* means to do something "wrongly," and *pre-* means "before" by talking about the words in each category. Students should know the meaning of *precious* and should be able to see that there is no base word whose meaning is changed by the prefix as there is in the other words. After discussing the meaning of the prefixes and how the prefixes change the meaning of the base word, revisit the word *misspell*. Help the students see that one *s* is part of the prefix and the other *s* is part of the base word, so both must be there. This will help them remember how to spell the word.

dis-	mis-	pre-	oddball
disagree	**misspell**	**preschool**	precious
dislike	mistreat	prefix	
disable	mismatch	premature	
disobey	misplace	preteen	
discover	misbehave	preview	
dishonest	misjudge	preheat	
disloyal		pretest	
disappear		precaution	
discomfort			

Extend

The game *Prefix Spin*, described in *WTW*, is recommended to review the prefixes in these first two sorts (*re-*, *un-*, *dis-*, *mis-*, and *pre-*). Students will be able to see how the same base words and prefixes can be used in many different combinations to form words with meanings that they can understand. The base word *cover*, for example, can be used to form *recover*, *uncover*, and *discover*.

SORT 47   PREFIXES (*EX-*, *NON-*, *IN-*, AND *FORE-*)

Introduce this sort in a manner similar to sort 45. The prefix *ex-* has subtle variations but generally means "out" in these words. *Non-* means "not," and *fore-* means "before" or "in front of." The prefix *in-* has two distinct meanings: "not" as in *incomplete* and "in" or "into" as in *indent*. Explain to your students that these words are all made up of prefixes but that the rest of the word is not always a base word that stands alone. For example, they will know that *exit* means to "go out" even though -*it* does not have a related meaning. Students will know the meaning of *indenting* a paragraph. They might be interested in learning that *dent* is related to *dentist* and *dental* coming from the Latin word for tooth. In a sense when they *indent* they take a bite into the paragraph.

ex-	non-	in-	fore-
exit	**nonsense**	**incomplete**	**forecast**
extend	nonfiction	incorrect	forearm
extra	nonstop	indecent	forehead
express	nonfat	(in)	foresee
exclude			foreshadow
exclaim		indent	foremost
expand		insight	
		income	
		indoor	

SORT 48   PREFIXES (*UNI-*, *BI-*, *TRI-*, AND OTHER NUMBERS)

Introduce this sort in a manner similar to other sorts in this unit. Students will learn that *uni-* means "one," *bi-* means "two," *tri-* means "three," *quad-* means "four," *pent-* means "five," and *oct-* means "eight." Explain that in ancient calendars October was the eighth month, unlike the modern calendar in which it is the tenth month.

uni-	bi-	tri-	other
unicycle	**bicycle**	**tricycle**	**quadrangle**
unity	biweekly	trilogy	pentagon
unicorn	bisect	triangle	octagon
unique	bilingual	triple	octopus
union		triplet	October
unison		tripod	
uniform		trio	
universe			

Extend and Review

Draw attention to the word *bilingual* and find out how many students you have who are or know someone who is bilingual. Remind students of words they studied earlier, like *penguin* and *language*, in which the *gu* had the sound of /gw/.

SORT 49   SUFFIXES (-Y, -LY, AND -ILY)

Demonstrate

In this sort and the ones that follow attention shifts to the suffixes. Prepare a set of words to use for teacher-directed modeling. Save the discussion of word meanings until after sorting. Display a transparency of the words on the overhead or hand out the sheet of words to the students. Ask the students what they notice about the words and get ideas about how the words can be sorted. Students might note that all the words end in *y* and contain base words that they recognize. Put up the headers and key words and then sort the rest of the words. Introduce the term **suffix** as a part that is added to the end of a word. Help students think about what the final -*y*, -*ly*, and -*ily* do to the words by talking about the meaning and use of the words. Summarize by explaining that -*y* turns a noun like *sun* into an adjective that means "like the sun" or "having sun," while -*ly* and -*ily* turn adjectives like *slow* into adverbs that describe "how" something is done or "the manner in which" something is done. (In the case of *daily* and *nightly*, -*ly* indicates "when.") Students might add these terms to the headers as reminders.

Sort, Check, and Reflect

Have students repeat the sort using the same headers and key words. To reinforce the idea of the base words you might suggest underlining them. This will raise questions about the base word in *happily*, for example, and how it was changed before adding -*ly*. Have students write in the base word for the -*ily* words since they cannot simply underline them. Encourage the students to reflect by asking them how the words in each column are alike and what they have learned about adding -*y* and -*ly* to base words.

-y (having / like)	-ly (in the manner of)	-ly (in the manner of)
sunny	**slowly**	**happily**
rainy	quickly	easily
foggy	clearly	angrily
snowy	dimly	lazily
misty	quietly	noisily
stormy	loudly	
chilly	daily	
cloudy	roughly	
windy	smoothly	
breezy		

Extend and Review

To review parts of speech create frame sentences such as: *Today is* ____. and *He walked* ____. Ask students to find adjectives that describe the noun *today* and adverbs that modify the verb *walk*.

Review with students how to add *-ing* and *-ed* to words like *dig*. Ask them to find two words in the sort that had to double the final letter before adding a suffix (*sunny, foggy*). Point out that the word *dim* did not have to double before adding *-ly* because it does not begin with a vowel. Review how to form the plural of words like *party* and *baby* (change the *y* to *i* and add *es*) and how to make the past tense of words like *carry* and *fly* (change the *y* to *i* and add *ed*). Ask them to find words in the sort that also had to change the *y* to *i* (this includes *daily*). Help them articulate a new rule about adding *-ly* to words that end in *y*.

Give students transfer words to practice applying the rules. Ask them to add *-y* or *-ly* to the following base words: *bog (boggy), run (runny), nip (nippy), bug (buggy), dust (dusty), bump (bumpy), soap (soapy), kind (kindly), bad (badly), nice (nicely), busy (busily), hasty (hastily), hungry (hungrily)*.

Review antonyms by asking students to find opposites among the words in this sort: *slowly/quickly, clearly/dimly, quietly/loudly, smoothly/roughly*. Have students look for weather words: *foggy, sunny, rainy, snowy, misty, stormy, chilly, cloudy, windy, breezy*.

SORT 50   COMPARATIVES (*-ER* AND *-EST*)

Introduce this sort in a manner similar to sort 49, reviewing the term **suffix.** Sort first by *-er* and *-est* and talk about the meaning of the words and what the suffix does to the base word. (When comparing two things *-er* is used. When comparing more than two things use *-est*.) Ask students to underline the base words to highlight the fact that the base word in *happier* or *happiest* has been changed. Sort these words into two new categories under *-ier* and *-iest*. Ask the students to form a generalization that covers these words and remind them of previous sorts. Add to the generalization you formed with sort 47 (when a word ends in *y*, change the *y* to *i* before adding *-ly*, *-ed*, *-es*, *-er*, or *-est*).

-er	*-est*	*-ier*	*-iest*
braver	**bravest**	**happier**	**happiest**
calmer	calmest	easier	easiest
closer	closest	prettier	prettiest
fewer	fewest	crazier	craziest
cooler	coolest	dirtier	dirtiest
hotter	hottest		
weaker	weakest		

Extend

To review the rules involved in adding suffixes sort the words as shown below:

double	*e*-drop	**change *y* to *i***	**nothing**
hotter	braver	happier	calmer
	closer	easier	fewer
		prettier	cooler
		crazier	weaker
		dirtier	

To help students **transfer** their understanding of these rules to new words ask them to add *-er* and *-est* to these words: *fat, safe, fine, lucky*.

SORT 51   SUFFIXES (-*NESS*, -*FUL*, AND -*LESS*)

Students should be able to do this as a student-centered sort and establish the categories for themselves. Discuss with students how suffixes change the meaning and use of the word. The suffix -*ness* creates nouns out of adjectives and suggests a "state of being." The suffixes -*ful* and -*less* create adjectives that mean "full of" or "having," and "without."

Draw students' attention to the base words and ask them to find any that have been changed before adding these suffixes. They should see that words ending in a consonant or *e* simply add the endings that start with consonants and do not require any such changes. However, base words that end in *y* must change the *y* to *i* (*happiness*, *plentiful*, and *penniless*).

-*ness*	-*ful*	-*less*	combination of suffixes
darkness	**graceful**	**homeless**	**carelessness**
goodness	colorful	hopeless	thankfulness
weakness	faithful	worthless	helplessness
illness	thoughtful	restless	peacefulness
kindness	painful	penniless	
happiness	fearful	harmless	
	dreadful		
	plentiful		

Extend

Have students cut apart the base word and suffixes and recombine them to create even more words: *homeless/homelessness, faithful/faithfulness, hopeless/hopelessness*; and to create antonym pairs like *careless/careful, painful/painless, fearful/fearless*. Additional words include: *thankless, thoughtless, painless, fearless, careless, useless, hopeful, restful, helpful, harmful, usefulness, powerless, thoughtfulness, hopelessness, helplessness,* and so on.

SPELL CHECK 7 ASSESSMENT FOR AFFIXES

Retention Test

The words below have been selected from previous lessons. (You may want to use different ones.) Call them aloud for students to spell on a sheet of notebook paper and then ask the students to rewrite them into categories and explain why they grouped them together.

1. prefix
2. bisect
3. uneven
4. prettiest
5. octagon
6. disloyal
7. carelessness
8. unicorn
9. expand
10. review
11. triangle
12. misspell
13. quickly
14. dirtier
15. incorrect
16. bravest
17. forehead
18. faithful
19. nonsense
20. noisily

re-	*un-*	*oddball*
rebuild	**unable**	recopy
unbeaten	recycle	unwrap
refill	unselfish	refinish
remodel	retrace	uncle
unhappy	unkind	retake
return	review	unpack
unfair	uneven	rewrite
reptile	unequal	unbutton

dis-	mis-	pre-
disagree	misspell	preschool
mistreat	dislike	prefix
disable	premature	mismatch
preteen	misplace	discover
preview	dishonest	preheat
disloyal	misbehave	precious
discomfort	pretest	disobey
disappear	misjudge	precaution

ex-	non-	in-	fore-
exit	nonsense	incomplete	
forecast	extend	incorrect	
forearm	nonfiction	extra	
express	forehead	indecent	
foresee	exclude	foreshadow	
exclaim	indent	nonstop	
insight	income	expand	
nonfat	foremost	indoor	

uni-	*bi-*	*tri-*	other
unicycle	**bicycle**	**tricycle**	
quadrangle	unity	biweekly	
trilogy	pentagon	unicorn	
bisect	unique	triangle	
union	octagon	universe	
octopus	unison	triple	
uniform	triplet	October	
tripod	bilingual	trio	

-y	-ly	-ily
sunny	**slowly**	**happily**
quickly	rainy	clearly
snowy	easily	foggy
dimly	misty	quietly
stormy	loudly	angrily
daily	chilly	cloudy
windy	noisily	breezy
roughly	lazily	smoothly

Words Their Way: Word Sorts for Syllables and Affixes Spellers © 2005 by Prentice-Hall, Inc.

-er	-est	-ier	-iest
braver	**bravest**		**happier**
happiest	calmer		easier
calmest	prettier		closer
fewest	easiest		craziest
fewer	closest		cooler
crazier	hotter		prettiest
coolest	weakest		hottest
dirtier	weaker		dirtiest

-*ness*	-*ful*	-*less*	Combinations of suffixes
darkness	graceful		homeless
carelessness	goodness		colorful
thoughtful	faithful		hopeless
thankfulness	painful		weakness
helplessness	illness		restless
harmless	worthless		kindness
peacefulness	penniless		fearful
happiness	plentiful		dreadful

Words Their Way: Word Sorts for Syllables and Affixes Spellers © 2005 by Prentice-Hall, Inc.

SORTS 52-55

Miscellaneous Sorts

NOTES FOR THE TEACHER

The four sorts in this section are something of a miscellaneous collection that explores different features of words. They are included here at the end of the syllables and affixes stage because many of the words require a more sophisticated vocabulary than words in earlier sorts. However, teachers can use their own judgment about using these sorts earlier in the sequence if they feel it is appropriate.

Homophones are first introduced in the within word pattern stage and are revisited here with two-syllable words in sort 52. Chapter 6 in *WTW* describes games and other resources that can be used with this sort. The spelling demons *they're, there*, and *their* are included again even though they were first introduced in the within word pattern stage. **Homographs** are words that are spelled alike but are pronounced differently. Easy homographs often change the sound of the vowel to change the meaning (e.g., I *read* yesterday and I will *read* today. The man with the *bow* tie took a *bow*). The words in sort 53 vary in meaning according to which syllable is accented (e.g., We plan to *record* a *record*).

Sort 54 looks at words with the *ei* pattern to explore the generalization that the order of letters for the long *-e* sound is "*i* before *e* except after *c*." This sort is included here rather than earlier with other vowel patterns because many of the words that follow the generalization, such as *deceive* and *conceit*, are words more appropriate for older students.

Sorting words by syllables in sort 55 is placed here to serve as a bridge to the longer words explored in the derivational relations stage and because it includes words more appropriate for upper elementary and middle grades. In this sort the names of the continents are included as words often assigned for spelling in the upper grades. The word *Europe* repeats from earlier.

SORT 52   HOMOPHONES

Demonstrate, Sort, and Reflect

There are 27 words in this week's sort, but some of them repeat from earlier sorts (*choose, flower, higher, very*, and *weather*). No headers are provided since the sorting activity consists of matching word pairs. Present a pair of words like *berry* and *bury*. Ask students what they notice about them (they sound alike but are spelled differently). If students do not know the term **homophone**, supply the word. Continue to pair up words and to talk about what the words mean. Students will typically know one homophone better than the other, but by pairing them up to compare spelling and by discussing their meaning the new words will become familiar.

Ask students for ideas about how certain spellings can be remembered: *Sellers* have *sales* while *cellers* might have jail *cells*; *there* has the little word *here* as in "here and there"; one of the *s*'s deserted in *desert*; your *principal* is a *pal*, and so on.

berry	bury	vary	very	
cellar	seller	hire	higher	
weather	whether	desert	dessert	
allowed	aloud	principle	principal	
flour	flower	chews	choose	
bored	board	merry	marry	
		they're	there	their

Extend

Draw small pictures on word cards or in word study notebooks to stimulate memory for the meaning of the word (e.g., draw a strawberry for *berry* and a tombstone for *bury*). Also, have students use these words in sentences. Pairs of students might be assigned 3–6 words and asked to compose sentences. They might be challenged to make up sentences that contain both of the words such as: *I was not sure <u>whether</u> the <u>weather</u> would be good enough to plan a party outdoors.* The students can share these sentences with each other orally.

The game of *Homophone Solitaire* is described in Chapter 7 of *WTW*. *Homophone Rummy* and *Win, Lose, or Draw*, described in Chapter 6 of *WTW*, will review and extend the study of homophones. *Memory* or *Concentration* would work well also. These games may substitute for no-peeking or blind sorts since these cannot be done without any categories.

SORT 53   HOMOGRAPHS

Demonstrate, Sort, Check, and Reflect

In these words the accented syllable is in bold type. Stressed syllables can also be marked with accent marks or underlined. Begin by writing up a sentence such as: *He will present you with a present.* Ask students what they notice about the words *pre sent'* and *pres' ent.* They should note that the words are spelled the same but sound slightly different. Review with students words such as *wind, lead,* and *read* and introduce the term **homograph**, which means "same writing" or "same spelling." (You might point out how this term is related to *homophone*, which means "same sound.") Go back to the sentence and ask students to identify the part of speech for each word and place the words under the headers *noun* and *verb*. Proceed in a similar manner with each set of words, using them in sentences or inviting students to use them and then to sort them under the headings. When all the words have been sorted read down each column, placing extra emphasis on the accented syllable. Ask students what they notice. (The nouns are accented on the first syllable and the verbs on the second syllable.)

noun	verb
present	pre**sent**
desert	de**sert**
record	re**cord**
permit	per**mit**
rebel	re**bel**
object	ob**ject**

subject	sub**ject**
reject	rej**ect**
produce	pro**duce**
conduct	con**duct**
export	ex**port**
contract	con**tract**

Extend

Students should work with these words using standard weekly routines, but partners in a no-peeking or blind sort will have to pronounce the words carefully and perhaps use them in a sentence before asking their buddy to sort them by stress. Ask students to work together to create sentences for these words and to record some of these sentences in their word study notebooks. Students might also draw small pictures as described for homophones above. The game of *Homograph Concentration*, described in Chapter 7, is very appropriate for review.

SORT 54   *I* BEFORE *E* EXCEPT AFTER *C*

Demonstrate

This is best done as a teacher-directed sort because it involves several steps. Begin by going over the words to pronounce and talk about the meaning of any words students might not know. Next, model a **sound sort** by putting up the key words *thief* and *neighbor*. Ask students to listen for the vowel sound in each word (long -*e* and long -*a*), and then sort the rest of the words with the students' help by the sound of the vowel in the accented syllable. The word *mischief* will be an oddball. Next, ask the students to look for the pattern of letters that spells the vowel sound. Use *thief* and *seize* as key words for long -*e* and sort the rest of the words under them. Explain that not knowing whether to use *ie* or *ei* makes these words difficult to spell correctly because the sound is the same. However, there is one thing that will help. Ask the students to look for words in which the *ei* comes after the letter *c*. Put these words in another column and put up the headers. The sort will now look something like the following:

ie = long -*e*	*ei* = long -*e*	*cei* = long -*e*	*ei* = long -*a*	oddball
thief	**seize**	**receive**	**neighbor**	mischief
niece	weird	ceiling	eighteen	
priest	either	deceive	weigh	
grief	neither	conceit	sleigh	
shield		receipt	freight	
relieve			reign	
yield				
belief				

Sort, Check, and Reflect

After modeling the sort have students cut apart and shuffle their own cards and sort them using the same headers and key words. Get students to talk about the categories in their own words and then introduce the old rule: *i* before *e* except after *c* and when sounded as *a* as in *neighbor* and *weigh*. Talk about how well this rule covers the words in the sort. (It does not account for the words under *seize*.) Explain that the rule does help spellers to remember how to spell the words that have *cei*, but we just have to memorize how to spell the others.

Extend

Standard weekly routines that include blind sorts or no-peeking sorts will give students practice in mastering these words. Word hunts will not turn up much because there are really only a small number of words spelled with *ei* and *ie*. A few more include *deceit, eight, eighty,* and *leisure.*

SORT 55   SYLLABLE SORT

Students will sort these words by the number of syllables. Expect some disagreement about words like *temperature*. After modeling several words under each header turn the sorting over to the students. Identify any syllables that might be challenging to spell (such as the last syllable in *Australia*). Help students see that careful pronunciations of words like *temperature* will help them spell the word. Ask students to pull out the words that name continents and note the similar spelling in the last syllable of *Africa, America,* and *Antarctica*. (Note that *America* needs *North* and *South* added to name the two continents in the Western Hemisphere.) Read the words to identify the stressed syllable and have students mark the syllable by underlining it on their word cards. Use the dictionary to resolve disputes and introduce the idea of primary and secondary accent in words with more than two syllables.

Two syllables	Three syllables	Four syllables
ocean	**continent**	**information**
island	example	especially
Europe	animal	America
building	Australia	population
ancient	important	necessary
Asia	beautiful	temperature
	hemisphere	Antarctica
	remember	unusual
	Africa	variety

Extend

Challenge students to find more four-syllable words, or even five-syllable words in word hunts. The game of *Stressbusters* or any follow-the-path game board can be adapted to reinforce syllabication. Students move around the board according to the number of syllables they can count in the word cards they draw.

berry	bury	cellar
very	seller	flour
weather	bored	vary
hire	desert	board
flower	whether	principle
chews	higher	aloud
allowed	dessert	principal
merry	choose	marry
they're	there	their

noun	verb	
present	present	desert
record	permit	rebel
permit	desert	record
rebel	subject	object
reject	object	subject
produce	conduct	export
conduct	reject	produce
contract	export	contract

ie = /e/	cei = /e/	ei = /e/	ei = /a/
thief	**receive**		**neighbor**
seize	niece		ceiling
eighteen	weigh		priest
deceive	weird		sleigh
grief	shield		either
receipt	mischief		relieve
yield	belief		freight
neither	reign		conceit

Words Their Way: Word Sorts for Syllables and Affixes Spellers © 2005 by Prentice-Hall, Inc.

Two syllables	Three syllables	Four syllables
ocean	**continent**	**information**
variety	Antarctica	example
Asia	unusual	population
building	America	remember
animal	hemisphere	necessary
ancient	important	Australia
Europe	Africa	temperature
especially	island	beautiful

Words Their Way: Word Sorts for Syllables and Affixes Spellers © 2005 by Prentice-Hall, Inc.

Appendix

Blank Word Sort Template

Word Work at Home Form

Word Sort Corpus (numbers indicate which sort the words appear in)

Blank Sort Template

Words Their Way: Word Sorts for Syllables and Affixes Spellers © 2005 by Prentice-Hall, Inc.

WORD WORK AT HOME

Name _____ Date _____

Cut apart your words and sort them first. Then write your words below under a key word.

_____

_____

_____

_____

_____

_____

_____

_____

_____

_____

What did you learn about words from this sort?

_____

_____

_____

On the back of this paper write the same key words you used above. Ask someone to shuffle your word cards and call them aloud as you write them into categories. Look at each word as soon as you write it. Correct it if needed.

Check off what you did and ask a parent to sign below.
_____ Sort the words again in the same categories you did in school.
_____ Write the words in categories as you copy the words.
_____ Do a no-peeking sort with someone at home.
_____ Write the words into categories as someone calls them aloud.
_____ Find more words in your reading that have the same sound and/or pattern. Add them to the categories on the back.
Signature of Parent _____

Words Their Way: Word Sorts for Syllables and Affixes Spellers © 2005 by Prentice-Hall, Inc.

Word Sort Corpus

able	31	antique	42	battle	31	bridle	31
aboard	37	anyone	13	beautiful	55	brief	1
about	24	anything	13	beauty	22	brightly	20
acted	5	appear	30	because	37	broken	36
acted	18	apple	31	before	27	brother	33
actor	34	appoint	24	beggar	34	brought	43
actress	39	approach	21	begging	4	brushes	7
adding	4	April	32	begun	37	buckle	41
address	39	apron	36	belief	54	budget	39
adhere	30	area	17	believe	37	bugle	31
adore	27	argue	40	below	21	building	55
advice	20	armies	10	benches	7	bureau	21
afraid	37	around	24	beneath	37	burglar	34
Africa	55	arrive	20	berries	10	bury	52
after	33	ashes	7	berry	52	busy	14
again	37	ashore	27	beside	13	butter	15
against	37	Asia	55	better	34	cabin	36
agreed	37	ask	2	between	37	cable	31
airplane	26	asking	2	beware	26	called	5
all right	25	assignment	43	beyond	37	calmer	50
alleys	10	athlete	17	bicycle	48	calmest	50
allow	24	attack	41	bigger	34	cancel	32
allowed	52	attic	41	bilingual	48	candies	10
almost	25	auction	25	birdbath	29	candle	31
alone	21	August	25	birthday	29	captain	36
aloud	37	Australia	55	bisect	48	capture	35
aloud	52	author	25	biweekly	48	career	30
alphabet	44	autumn	25	blanket	15	careful	26
already	25	avoid	24	bled	6	carelessness	51
also	25	awake	19	bleed	6	carpet	26
although	25	aware	26	board	52	carried	11
always	25	awesome	25	body	9	carries	11
amaze	19	awful	25	bookcase	12	carrying	11
America	55	awhile	37	bookmark	12	cartoon	22
among	37	awkward	25	bookworm	12	castle	43
amount	24	awoke	21	border	27	catalogue	40
amuse	22	babies	10	bored	52	catcher	35
ancient	55	backward	28	bottle	31	cattle	32
angel	32	bacon	36	bottom	15	caught	44
angle	32	balloon	22	bought	43	caution	25
angrily	49	bandage	39	bowling	21	ceiling	54
angry	9	banquet	42	boys	10	cellar	52
animal	55	barber	26	bracelet	19	cement	38
announce	24	barefoot	26	branches	7	central	38
annoy	24	barely	26	brave	1	century	38
another	37	bargain	36	braver	50	cereal	38
answer	43	basement	19	bravest	50	certain	29
Antarctica	55	basket	15	breezy	49	changes	7

chapter	15	conquer	42	darkness	51	double	24
checkout	13	contain	19	daughter	44	downhill	12
cheerful	30	contest	38	daylight	12	downpour	12
chewing	4	continent	55	debate	37	downstairs	12
chews	52	contract	53	decay	19	downtown	12
chicken	41	control	17	deceive	54	dragon	36
chief	1	cookbook	12	decide	20	draw	6
children	17	cookie	9	declare	26	dreadful	51
chilly	49	cooler	50	decode	21	dream	3
chimney	9	coolest	50	deer	8	dreamer	34
chocolate	19	copied	11	defeat	23	dreaming	3
choose	52	copies	11	defend	37	dreary	30
chorus	27	copying	11	degree	37	drew	6
chosen	36	corncob	27	delight	20	drive	6
churches	7	corner	27	depend	37	driver	34
cider	38	correct	38	describe	20	driveway	20
circle	38	cotton	36	desert	52	dropped	5
cities	10	cougar	22	desert	53	drove	6
clean	3	cough	44	design	43	drowsy	24
cleaning	3	countdown	12	desire	37	during	29
cleaning	18	counter	24	despair	26	duties	10
clearly	49	country	24	dessert	52	dwarf	28
clog	1	county	24	destroy	24	early	30
close	3	couple	32	develop	37	earthquake	30
closed	5	courage	39	dialogue	40	easier	50
closely	21	cousin	36	diet	17	easiest	50
closer	50	cover	33	dimly	49	easily	49
closest	50	coward	24	diner	14	eastern	23
closing	3	cradle	31	dinner	14	easy	16
cloudy	49	crashes	7	direct	37	eat	3
cocoon	22	crayon	19	dirtier	50	eating	3
collar	33	crazier	50	dirtiest	50	editor	34
collect	38	craziest	50	dirty	29	eighteen	54
college	38	crazy	14	disable	46	either	54
color	33	create	17	disagree	46	electric	41
colorful	51	creator	34	disappear	46	elephant	44
combine	20	creature	35	discomfort	46	eleven	36
coming	4	cried	11	discover	46	employ	24
common	38	cries	11	dishonest	46	empty	9
compare	26	cruel	17	dislike	46	English	17
compass	39	crying	11	disloyal	46	enjoyed	11
compete	23	culture	35	disobey	46	enjoying	11
complain	19	curtain	36	distance	39	enjoys	11
complete	17	custom	38	ditches	7	enough	44
complex	41	cutting	4	divide	37	equal	42
compose	21	cyclist	38	doctor	33	equator	42
conceit	54	daily	49	dollar	33	equip	42
conclude	22	dairy	26	dolphin	44	equipment	42
conduct	53	dancer	34	donkeys	10	erode	21
confuse	22	danger	35	doodle	22	escape	19

especially	55	finish	16	gawking	25	headlight	12
Europe	21	fireflies	10	geese	8	headphones	12
Europe	55	firmly	29	general	38	headstrong	12
even	14	fixing	4	genius	38	healthy	23
every	9	flashlight	12	gentle	38	heaven	36
everyone	13	flavor	33	get	2	heavy	23
everything	13	flawless	25	getting	2	hello	14
evil	32	floated	18	getting	18	helped	5
example	55	floating	6	gingerbread	38	helplessness	51
exclaim	47	florist	27	giraffe	38	hemisphere	55
exclude	47	flour	52	gloves	7	hermit	30
excuse	22	flower	33	gnawed	25	herself	13
exit	47	flower	52	goalie	9	hidden	36
expand	47	foggy	49	golden	38	higher	20
explain	19	follow	15	goodness	51	higher	52
explode	21	foot	8	goose	8	highway	17
explore	27	forearm	47	gossip	38	highway	20
export	53	forecast	47	grabbed	5	hiking	4
express	47	forehead	47	graceful	51	himself	13
extend	47	foremost	47	grammar	33	hire	52
extra	47	foresee	47	grief	54	hockey	9
extreme	23	foreshadow	47	grinning	4	homeless	51
eyelashes	7	forest	27	guard	40	homophone	44
fabric	41	forgive	20	guess	40	honest	43
faded	18	forty	27	guesses	7	honey	9
failure	35	forward	27	guest	40	honor	43
fairy	26	fossil	32	guidance	40	hoped	5
faithful	51	fought	6	guide	40	hopeless	51
families	10	fought	44	guilty	40	hoping	18
farmer	34	fountain	36	guitar	40	hopped	5
fasten	43	foxes	7	gutter	38	hopping	18
father	33	fragile	32	gymnast	38	horses	7
fatigue	40	freedom	23	haircut	26	hostess	21
faucet	25	freight	54	halfway	17	hotter	50
favor	33	frequent	42	hammock	41	hottest	50
favorite	20	fresher	34	handle	31	human	16
fearful	51	frighten	20	happen	15	humming	4
feather	23	front	1	happier	50	humor	16
feature	23	frozen	16	happiest	50	hundred	17
feeling	4	fruit	1	happily	49	hungry	9
feet	8	furnish	29	happiness	51	hunted	5
female	15	further	29	happy	14	hunted	18
fever	15	future	35	harbor	33	hurried	11
fewer	50	gadget	39	hardly	26	hurries	11
fewest	50	gallon	36	harmless	51	hurry	29
fifteen	23	garage	38	harvest	26	hurrying	11
fifty	9	garbage	39	haunted	25	iceberg	40
figure	35	garden	26	having	4	idea	17
final	32	gather	38	headache	12	ignore	27
finger	15	gauge	40	headfirst	12	illness	51

important	55	laughed	25	matter	15	mouse	8
include	22	laughter	44	maybe	19	movie	9
income	47	laundry	25	mayor	19	moving	4
incomplete	47	lawyer	25	meaning	23	muscle	31
incorrect	47	lazily	49	measure	35	mushroom	17
increase	23	lazy	16	meet	3	music	16
indecent	47	leader	16	meeting	3	myself	13
indeed	23	leaf	8	meeting	18	named	5
indent	47	league	40	member	15	napkin	36
index	41	leaking	18	mercy	30	nature	35
indoor	47	learner	30	merely	30	naughty	44
inform	27	leashes	7	mermaid	29	nearby	30
injure	35	leather	23	merry	29	necessary	55
inquire	42	leaves	8	merry	52	needed	18
inside	13	leisure	35	message	39	needle	23
insight	47	lemon	16	metal	32	neighbor	54
inspect	17	lesson	14	metric	41	neither	54
intrigue	40	letter	14	mice	8	nephew	44
invite	20	level	32	middle	31	nervous	29
island	55	life	8	midget	39	never	16
itself	13	lighthouse	12	minute	16	nickel	41
jewel	32	lightning	20	mirror	33	niece	54
jockey	9	lightweight	12	misbehave	46	ninety	20
jogger	34	liked	5	mischief	54	nodded	5
jogging	4	lion	17	misjudge	46	nodded	18
joined	5	liquid	42	mismatch	46	noisily	49
journal	32	listen	43	misplace	46	noisy	24
journeys	10	little	31	mission	36	nonfat	47
July	9	lived	5	misspell	46	nonfiction	47
jump	2	lives	8	mistake	19	nonsense	47
jumping	2	living	4	mistreat	46	nonstop	47
jungle	31	loaf	8	misty	49	noodle	22
keep	6	loafer	21	mitten	36	normal	27
kept	6	loaves	8	mixed	5	northern	27
kernel	30	local	32	mixes	7	nothing	13
kindness	51	lonely	21	mixture	35	notice	39
kingdom	17	lonesome	21	moan	3	novel	32
kisses	7	loudly	49	moaning	3	number	15
kitchen	17	lower	21	model	32	obey	19
kitten	14	loyal	24	moisture	24	object	53
knew	6	luggage	39	moment	15	ocean	55
knife	8	machine	20	money	9	octagon	48
knives	8	magic	41	monkeys	10	October	48
know	6	mail	3	monster	17	octopus	48
knowledge	43	mailing	3	moody	22	office	39
knuckle	43	manage	39	morning	27	often	43
ladies	10	many	9	mosquito	42	older	34
ladybug	40	marble	26	mother	33	open	14
language	40	market	26	motor	33	order	27
later	14	marry	52	mountain	36	orphan	44

outside	13	pillow	15	pumpkin	17	reign	54
over	14	pilot	16	puppy	14	reject	53
owner	21	pitcher	35	purple	29	relax	41
package	39	places	7	purpose	29	relieve	54
paddle	31	plague	40	pushing	4	rely	9
painful	51	planet	16	put	2	remain	19
painter	19	planned	5	putting	2	remember	55
paper	14	plastic	41	quadrangle	48	remodel	45
parade	19	plays	10	quaint	42	remote	21
paragraph	44	pleasant	23	quality	42	repair	26
pardon	26	pleasure	35	quarrel	28	repeat	23
parents	26	plentiful	51	quarter	28	replied	11
parties	10	plenty	9	queasy	42	replies	11
partner	26	plot	1	question	42	replying	11
pass	2	plotting	18	quick	41	report	27
passed	5	pocket	41	quickly	49	reptile	45
passing	2	poet	17	quietly	49	request	42
pasture	35	poison	24	quit	1	require	42
pattern	15	police	39	quizzes	42	resign	43
pavement	19	polite	20	quotation	42	rest	2
payment	19	pollute	22	quote	1	resting	2
peacefulness	51	ponies	10	quoted	18	restless	51
peaches	7	population	55	rabbit	14	retake	45
peanut	16	postage	21	raccoon	22	retrace	45
pearly	30	poster	21	racquet	42	return	45
pencil	32	posture	35	railroad	19	review	45
penguin	36	practice	39	rainbow	19	reward	27
penniless	51	precaution	46	rainy	49	rewrite	45
penny	14	precious	46	raisin	19	rhyme	43
pentagon	48	prefix	46	rancher	35	rhythm	43
people	23	preheat	46	rather	33	ribbon	36
perfect	29	premature	46	rattle	31	rifle	31
perform	27	preschool	46	reader	23	riot	17
perfume	22	present	16	reading	4	river	16
perhaps	29	present	53	ready	9	rooster	22
permit	53	pressure	35	reason	16	rough	44
perplex	41	preteen	46	rebel	53	roughly	49
person	29	pretest	46	rebuild	45	ruler	14
phantom	44	prettier	50	receipt	54	rumor	33
phone	1	prettiest	50	receive	54	run	2
photocopy	44	pretty	14	recess	39	running	2
photograph	44	preview	46	recopy	45	saddle	32
phrase	44	priest	54	record	27	said	6
physics	44	princess	39	record	53	sailor	34
pick	2	principal	52	recycle	45	sample	31
picking	2	principle	52	reduce	22	saucer	25
pickle	41	problem	15	refill	45	sausage	25
picnic	41	produce	22	refinish	45	saved	5
picture	35	produce	53	refuse	22	saving	18
pilgrim	17	provide	20	rehearse	30	say	6

scale	1	slept	6	steady	23	there	52
science	39	slid	6	stepped	5	thermos	30
scooter	22	slide	6	stolen	36	they're	52
scout	1	slightly	20	stomach	41	thief	54
scrapbook	12	slowly	49	stopping	4	thirsty	29
scratches	7	smaller	34	stories	10	thirteen	23
season	23	smell	1	stormy	49	thirty	29
second	16	smoother	34	stranger	34	though	43
seemed	5	smoothly	49	strong	40	thought	43
seize	54	sneaker	16	student	16	thoughtful	51
seller	52	snowflake	12	studied	11	thousand	24
senior	35	snowing	4	studies	11	threw	6
sentence	39	snowman	12	studying	11	through	43
sequel	42	snowplow	12	stupid	15	throughout	13
sequence	42	snowstorm	12	sturdy	29	throw	6
sermon	30	snowy	49	subject	53	Thursday	29
serpent	30	soapy	21	succeed	23	ticket	41
service	29	soften	43	sugar	33	tiger	14
setting	4	solar	33	summer	14	tiny	14
settle	31	somebody	13	sunlight	12	title	31
seven	16	somehow	13	sunny	49	toaster	21
severe	30	someone	13	super	14	today	19
shampoo	22	something	13	supper	14	tongue	40
sharp	1	sometime	13	suppose	21	tonight	20
sheep	8	somewhere	13	surgeon	39	tooth	8
shield	54	sooner	34	surprise	20	toothache	22
shine	6	sorry	27	survive	20	topic	41
shock	41	southern	24	swarm	28	torture	35
shone	6	spearmint	30	sweater	23	total	32
shorter	27	special	32	sweep	6	tough	44
shouted	5	speeches	7	swept	6	toward	26
shouting	18	spelling	4	swim	2	towel	32
shrug	40	spelling	18	swimmer	34	toys	10
sidewalk	20	spider	33	swimming	2	tractor	33
sideways	13	spirit	29	synagogue	40	trade	3
signal	32	splashes	7	table	31	trading	3
silent	15	squabble	28	taking	4	traffic	41
silver	33	squad	28	taking	18	trays	10
simple	31	squash	28	talking	4	treasure	35
sincere	30	squat	28	taught	44	treat	1
single	31	squirm	42	teacher	35	tremble	31
sister	15	squirrel	42	teardrop	30	trial	17
sit	2	stain	1	teeth	8	triangle	48
sitting	2	stand	2	telephone	44	tricycle	48
skate	3	standing	2	temperature	55	trilogy	48
skated	18	standing	18	thank	1	trio	48
skating	3	started	5	thankfulness	51	triple	48
sketches	7	stayed	11	their	52	triplet	48
sleep	6	staying	11	theme	1	tripod	48
sleigh	54	stays	11	themselves	13	trophy	44

trouble	24	unwrap	45	wardrobe	28	woman	8
trust	1	upon	37	warmth	28	women	8
try	9	use	3	warning	28	worker	28
Tuesday	22	useful	22	warrior	28	working	4
turkey	9	using	3	watch	28	world	28
turtle	29	using	18	watches	7	worry	28
twenty	9	vague	40	water	15	worse	28
twig	1	valleys	10	wave	3	worship	28
ugly	9	variety	55	waving	3	worthless	51
unable	45	vary	52	weaker	50	worthwhile	28
unbeaten	45	very	9	weakest	50	worthy	28
unbutton	45	very	52	weakness	51	wrap	1
uncle	45	video	17	weather	33	wreckage	43
unequal	45	village	39	weather	52	wrestle	43
uneven	45	violin	36	weigh	54	wrinkle	43
unfair	45	visit	16	weird	54	write	3
unhappy	45	visitor	34	when	1	writer	34
unicorn	48	voices	7	whether	52	writing	3
unicycle	48	voter	34	which	1	writing	18
uniform	48	vowel	32	whine	1	wrote	6
union	48	voyage	24	whistle	43	yearbook	30
unique	48	waffle	28	wife	8	yearn	30
unison	48	wagon	16	window	15	yell	2
unity	48	waited	5	windy	49	yelling	2
universe	48	waited	18	winter	15	yellow	15
unkind	45	wander	28	without	13	yield	54
unpack	45	wanted	5	wives	8	younger	34
unselfish	45	wanted	18	wolf	8	yourself	13
unusual	55	warden	28	wolves	8	zigzag	40